A St

Nancy Cleaves

Copyright © 2010 Nancy Cleaves
All rights reserved.
ISBN: 1453708049
ISBN-13: 9781453708040

Reprinted by Permission:

Rumi poems: translated by Coleman Barks.

Poems by Hakim Sanai printed in 'The Book of Everything; Journey of the Heart's Desire, Hakim Sanai's Walled Garden of Truth' by the Book Laboratory, © 2002, Andrews McMeel Publishing..

Quotes from Meister Eckhart, in 'Meditations with Meister Eckhart' by Matthew Fox, ©1983 by Bear & Company.

Quote from Hildegard of Bingen in 'Illuminations of Hildegard of Bingen', Text by Hildegard of Bingen with commentary by Matthew Fox, © 1985. Bear & Company.

See www.InnerTraditions.com

The Aramaic and translations in the chapter on Yeshua are from 'Prayers of the Cosmos' by Neil Douglas-Klotz.© 1990, HarperCollins, HarperSanFrancisco.

Regarded as Public Domain – Acknowledgement is given to Red Weeler/ Weiser for printing 'Songs of Kabir, A 15th Century Sufi Literary Classic, 2002.

Cover photo by Cate Brennan.

This book is dedicated

to the

children and youth of this generation.

We have handed you

an extremely heavy and grievous torch to bear.

May this story inspire and empower you

to restore *Malkutah: Heaven Here and Now*

Table of Contents

Acknowledgements — vii

Foreword to 'A Story to Live By' — ix

Introduction — xi

Part One: The Universe Story

The Beloved — 1

In the Beginning — 11

Keepers of the Sacred Tear — 29

Divine Human — 51

Part Two: Getting Back to the Story

The Witness of Abraham — 65

The Witness of Moses — 73

Yeshua, the embodiment of Hokhmah — 79

Part Three: The Soul's Journey

In the Tear	91
Chaos to Clarity	101
Invisible Heaven to Visible	115
Cosmic Illuminations	129
Creativity	127
Home	137
As it was in the Beginning is Now	147
References	155

Acknowledgements

*W*ithout the work of Neil Douglas-Klotz in his translations of Jesus' prayer and most quoted sayings from the Aramaic and Matthew Fox in founding the former University of Creation Spirituality, this story would have never been written. I give heartfelt thanks to these leaders, to all the teachers, especially Larry Edwards, to Art-as-Meditation facilitators, and to fellow students of UCS (now known as Wisdom University). To my editors Karen Murray and Marilynn Crow, thanks for gracious love and support, and dotting my 'eyes' with your gifts. Thanks to Wanda Shultz-Poole (theprismpatch) for sitting with this story (in its first phase), for a year on your own creative time and fashioning the stained glass icon (back cover). Reverent thanks to Coleman Barks for so quickly allowing me to reprint your translations of Rumi.

I have been graced with amazing friends and I thank you all for your continuous love and support. To Kathy Curtin my *anam cara*, soul friend in the Celtic tradition; thank-you for faithfully and prayerfully holding sacred space for me, and to MaryAnn Maruska, my soul sister, thank-you for keeping my flames of inspiration ignited. Thank-you Robert O'Hearn for all the long talks, and the love and kindness I feel across the miles. Thanks also to my many awesome friends who continually shower me with love and beauty: Marg and Stan Benner, Catherine Hamilton, Joyce Ferris (and all of my Temagami family), Laura and Gary Moon, Al and Yvette Paré, Nicole Taveres (also for the photo on the back cover), Tim Hegedus, John and Maritza Kent, Diane Warriner, Cathy Hewer, Karima Kassam and Jason Miller, Monica Himmelman, Tammy Becker, Cathy Walker, and all of my colleagues and students at St. Louis.

I am extremely grateful for the unique connection with my fellow Doctor of Ministry graduates in my area: Carol Kilby (Gaia Centre), Jake McArthur (Cairncrest), Barbara Susan Booth (Sacred Wisdom Centre), and MaryAnn Maruska (future spyder's web). It is such a joy to watch each other blossom, sharing our gifts for the betterment of all. One day we will have to rent a large tent for Cosmic Camp!

In the words of one of my sons, "I love you mom. I don't understand you but I love you." I thank my three sons, Nathan, Michael and Jonathan, their families, and many old friends for loving me, even though. To my dear grandchildren, I offer the thought, "This story is about you. You are all so precious." And to my brother, Paul, the one who has shown me true family love all of my life, enormous thanks. To the many other friends not named, thank-you for the gifts that you are.

Foreword to 'A Story to Live By'

Nancy Cleaves' book 'A Story to Live By' takes us back to a time before the telegraphic, sterilized speech of the mass media and Internet blogs, back to the language of story. If we listen to the story that she tells, we may change the way we act, and the way that the world continues.

The voice she chooses is that of Holy Wisdom, Sophia by her Greek name, Hokhmah by her ancient Hebrew one. The story she tells combines the mythic stories out of which Western culture arose---the Bible, creation stories, sayings of Jesus, wisdom of the Quran---but it also includes the most recent theories of scientific cosmology and cosmogony, the active speculations about the age-old questions: where did we come from, how, and why.

In the time before the "end of history" and before post-modern culture deemed only present fashion and present profit important, an older ethos endured. Cleaves' 'voice of Hokhmah' reminds us of this ethos. It reminds that, for there to be a planet for future generations, we need to place ourselves within a much larger caravan of ancestors, one in which more simple questions determined our actions. How do we leave a world for future humans? How do we help all of creation fulfill its destiny, not by ruling *over* the beings created before us, but by managing our planet *along* with them (the actual translation of Genesis 1:28).

In essence all really good stories are our own story.

This is one of them.

—Dr. Neil Douglas-Klotz

> To tell the story of anything,
>
> You must tell the story of everything.
>
> Thomas Berry

*T*he purpose of this writing is *one*. It is to accent the call back into harmony with one another and our Earth Home. We all breathe the same air; are nourished by one Mother Earth; there is one Sun that facilitates growth, warms our hearts, inspires solitude as it sets and guides the seasons; one Moon that sets the mighty tides. For those who are inspired to believe in a Higher Power seem to agree, essentially, that this Creator is Love and we are called to love and do no harm. Yet, we see harm everywhere. There is not one person, no matter what life circumstance, that doesn't grieve at the destruction caused by this oil spill, still gushing at the time of this writing, not to mention all of the wars and destruction that continue daily the world over.

A powerful quote by Albert Einstein says, 'The significant problems we face cannot be solved at the same level of thinking we were at when we created them.' If we are to find a solution and bring healing to our Earth and species, we cannot do it with the same thinking that has brought destruction. As I reflect on our history, I am convinced that dualistic thinking has given rise to a lot of our problems, and so a focus on unity and harmony can provide the framework and tools to get us to a future that is safe for all, and love and harmony can be expressed. Life is one.

One doesn't have to investigate far to see the poisonous view of dualism: spiritual is good and eternal while the physical is corrupt and temporal; heaven is a divine place where we will go when we die and Earth is a place that has been cursed because of human disobedience; saints and sinners (the categories change according to each religion and even sects within each.); God is up there and the human is down here; creation is dead matter and only humans are conscious; the community of human life is higher and more important than Earth; male is superior to female; civilized humans are greater than indigenous tribes; rich and poor; this group of people is entitled to this land, and not another; and some look for the solution to our disasters in one holy prophet who will come one day (again, the prophet changes according to each religion) and will separate the saved from the damned. The list goes on and on. This dualistic thinking breeds arrogance and justifies oppression and killing. For the most part, it serves those in power, whether it is the multi-billion dollar corporation that continues to deplete natural resources and destroy the environment, or one faction killing another for their own agenda. We have the fundamental stream of the three religions birthed from the ecology of the Middle East, either killing each other now, or looking to some judgement day that will kill everyone except their group, all because they have a special divine calling that excludes everyone else. And that small plot of land is, somehow, only *their* sacred place.

We could liken all of this dualistic thinking as a canal, made for one purpose; power over others by force or fund. Most of our social, economic, political and institutional systems can be likened to this canal. It is all about making money, as much and as quickly as possible and maintaining control. It is straight, rather boring, and its waters now murky and polluted. The wild life is gone. There are a few steam ships in this canal, a few yachts, smaller boats, but most people don't even have a raft. There are lots of dead bodies in it; those who ran out of breath or were run over.

There is another way of being in this global community. That way could be likened to a river. Everyone belongs on this river.

Its waters flow in unity and harmony. It is magnificent and majestic. The people are well aware that they did not make the river; it is a gift. Some take time to search for the Source, and It is called by many names, all in reverence. The waters are crystal clear, so much so that one can drink from it. Wildlife is abundant. The river is all about Beauty and adventure. What great experience lies just around the bend? This river operates on compassion. The canal people are claiming more and more of this river for their own gain. So as much as those on the river deserve to just enjoy the Beauty, they have to stand up and protect it before it is too late. This river is both visible and invisible, and has been flowing for almost 14 billion years. This writing is the story of the river.

Thomas Berry, who passed from us last year, dedicated his life to elevating our human consciousness by telling of the Universe as story. This Story touches the perimeters of our present awareness, and stretches it and stretches it, until there is no perimeter but the growing expanse of the vast Universe. This entire Universe is a tapestry of amazing beauty, and everything lives in connection and relationship to the whole. Embracing the Universe as story is nothing less than a mystical experience in divine compassion and awe.

We need a context as human beings, and the Universe Story provides us with a rich one. At one time we thought the Earth was flat and that informed our ways. Then, we discovered this solar system and our awareness grew. One picture that has sold more copies than any other is the first picture taken of Earth as a living planet, taken from Space in 1968. That has shifted our consciousness. Now we can view many of the 100 billion galaxies through the Hubble telescope. Scientists have discovered DNA, and the same four components of ATGC are coded in every living organism, in different orders and frequencies. If you could take one of your genes and inject it into a tree, the tree would not reject it as foreign, but would reassemble the order, add its own components, and make it a tree!

So from the smallest context of DNA exemplifying how we are so connected and so much the same, to the largest context of over 100 billion galaxies, there is a clear message of unity and harmony. Life is One. There is One Essence that flows and brings life; a great Wisdom at work. All of creation is one. In truth, we are the Universe becoming conscious of Itself. The more we awaken to this reality, the more we begin to realize the power and compassion that lies within. We are the beauty of this Universe in awakening consciousness. We are the sacred reflection of the Invisible. To become conscious of who we really are is celebration in itself. It addresses the age-old quest. Who are we? It heightens our sense of awe, empowers us, and fosters a sense of the sacred in Life, all Life. We, all Creation, are Life in unison. The running brook is you and you are the dance in the running brook. You are the fragrance in the blooming lotus.

The more this consciousness grows in us, the more we realize we are very ably equipped, on cosmic dimensions, to stop the death and destruction, and to restore and heal our Earth Home. The Wisdom, the creative Beauty that has been at work for 14 billion years to bring us this far, is still a cosmic resource bursting with energy to help us with this mammoth task, and to enlighten us to new ways of being that work for all. How quickly our body flows with healing at a single cut. Earth has been ravaged. Healing Wisdom calls to all of us to restore Beauty. As the 'Universe Story' tells us:

"Because creatures in the universe do not come from some place outside it, we only think of the universe as a place where qualities that will one day bloom are for the present hidden as dimensions of emptiness." (p.76)

What is waiting to be bloomed in each one of us? Most of us see ourselves as ordinary people, nothing to liken ourselves to Ghandi, or Mother Teresa. The thing that marks these great people and others is they had the courage and stamina to access those qualities available to all of us – every one of us! Those same qualities are eager to bloom in us. And to do the work at hand, it will take all of us.

This story is told from the voice of Wisdom (or 'Hokhmah' in Hebrew). At the top of the Tree of Life, beyond the abyss of where human consciousness can rise on its own is a triangle. Kether, is the crown at the top, Binah, which I refer to as Intelligent Beauty, and Hokhmah (Wisdom), form the two bases of the triangle.

Neil Douglas-Klotz is an Aramaic scholar and well-known author. He has translated the prayer, beatitudes, and popular sayings of Jesus, from his Native language, Aramaic. Neil's work would be of great value to anyone concerned with what the life of Jesus meant in his Middle Eastern context, and whatever he said, he said it in Aramaic, a language very different from Greek or English. Neil's research explains how many of Yeshua's early followers saw him as the embodiment of Hokhmah. This is another reason for choosing the Voice of Hokhmah, Wisdom, to tell the story. Leaving aside doctrinal debate and labels, this Essence of Wisdom is referred to in most religions.

The last section of this story is the telling of the Universe story as our soul's journey: From chaos, to clarity of light, invisible heaven to tangible heaven, and expressing our unique creativity in the fluidity of the divine feminine and the terrain of the sacred masculine. We go around the cosmic journey again and again and again, each time, coming Home to our true selves in deeper dimensions.

You see, deep in the crystal waters of this river of life is your true reflection. You don't recognize yourself in the beginning. It looks like the face of the purest and brightest angel. We are all blinded by our pain and our fears. Little by little, as we embark on our journey, attending to the needs of our soul, that reflection calls us, like an echo from an ancient place. Gradually, or sometimes suddenly, in a moment of quiet reverence, you look into these waters and recognize your own reflection. You see that you are beauty itself. You! You are radiance. You shine with the essence of an angel. And this - is your story.

So then, "Once upon a no-time . . . .

Unless otherwise specified, all prose and poems are by the author.

> Every story is true.
> And some of them actually happened.
>
> Celtic Storyteller

The Beloved

My name is Hokhmah, Holy Wisdom. To some I am known as Sophia, Ancient Wisdom, the Living Logos, Eternal Word. From before the Before, I am; and I am with the Beloved. I am the Way of peace and compassion. I am the Door to the realm of Sacred Mystery. I am that Renewable Life that sustains you. With my wisdom, I have fashioned the Universe. To find me is a Treasure beyond gold. I want to tell you a story. It is a story of unfolding compassion, enormous sacrifice, longing desire, yearning, and birthing; it is a story of One who is Love, Harmony and Beauty. This is the story of the Universe; it is your story. If you remember anything I tell you, remember this: It is one story. For all that is, comes forth from the One, and unto the One all return; in the Breath of the One, all breathe; in the Life of the One, all live.

My story begins with my Beloved. Hmm, how can I describe this One to you? The Universe tries to describe Her. Silent Compassion speaks her Name. This One is called by many names: God, Goddess, Allah, Alaha (Sacred Unity), Aum (All that Exists), Elohim (The One expressed in Many), Brahma, Creator, Va (Wow) and on and on, but in truth there are no names that can be given to this One. The Universe is not large enough to contain Her. There is no need small enough that doesn't move Her. When you listen to the Silence, She embraces you. I know Her well. Binah, Spirit of Intelligent Beauty, and I, have always been with Her. You could call us Love, Lover and Beloved. In Truth, It is Mystery.

This Beloved is neither male, nor female, nor other; and is altogether male, and female, and other. I will often refer to the Beloved as 'She', to try to balance all the maleness that has been attributed to the One for so many centuries. My wisdom is always about balance. And I will refer to the Beloved as 'It', for It is not made in man's image and is not a God only for the humans. It has created all things.

At the heart of all the holy prayers from every spiritual tradition is loving devotion. These prayers rise as sacred incense, adoring the Beloved for her generous Beauty.

※ ※ ※

From the heart of Judaism:

'Shema Israel, Adonnai, Elohanu, Adonnai, Ehud.'
'Hear, oh Israel, the Lord your God, the Lord is One.'

※ ※ ※

In the ancient Sanskrit language, Buddhists pray:

'Sri Ram, Jai Ram, Jai Jai Ram Aum, Sri Ram, Jai Ram, Jai Jai Ram Aum.'
'To All that exists, the only Being, God personal and impersonal, sun and moon, masculine and feminine, be always power.'

※ ※ ※

Hindus pray:

> 'Aum Tara, Tutara, Ture Soha.'
> 'To All that exists, the only Being, Healer of all brokenness, Remover of all fear, Bestower of all good fortune. May it be so.'

❀ ❀ ❀

A holy teacher in the Sikh faith had been in meditation for ten years, and experienced the Beloved in a flash. He said 'Va!' 'Wow!' For the Sikhs, the most holy mantra is:

> 'Vaahe-Guru'
> 'Wonderful – Enlightener.'

❀ ❀ ❀

The Christian prayer in Aramaic, the language of Yeshua, (Jesus) begins:

> 'Abwoon d'bashemaya'
> 'Oh Breathing Life, your Name shines everywhere.'

❀ ❀ ❀

The Muslims begin their prayer with:

> 'Bismillah Irahman Irahim'
> 'In the name of God, compassionate and merciful.'

❀ ❀ ❀

The Sufi prayer begins,

> 'Toward the One, the Perfection of Love, Harmony and Beauty, the only Being,'

❀ ❀ ❀

One of the many prayers in the Bahai tradition:

> 'Ultimate Reality, Unknowable Essence.'

A common Native prayer begins:

> 'Oh Great Spirit whose voice I hear in the winds and whose breath gives life to all the world – hear me.'

There are countless sacred prayers and all reveal the tender desire in the heart of every human being to return love and gratitude to such a majestic and generous Beloved. Every child, every man and every woman is called to be a seeker, and those that seek are found. You often call them mystics. Mystics span across generations, and are found in every spiritual tradition. And, of course, as the One they seek is the Only Beloved, their voices are in unison. They abound in love for the Beloved, and express a deep awe and wonder at the miracle of Life. Although they can't put their experience into words, their overwhelming love compels them to try. Meister Eckhart, a Christian mystic said that the sign of the new birth is that you see God everywhere. Martin Buber, a Jewish mystic and philosopher said that there is no God worth keeping, except the One that can't be kept. Gandhi, at the end of his life said that he was convinced that there was only one God and that God is Truth. I want you to hear the heart of just a few of these mystics..

O how may I ever express that secret word?
O how can I say He is not like this;
and He is like that?
If I say that He is within me, the universe is ashamed:
If I say He is without me, it is falsehood.
He makes the inner and the outer worlds to be indivisibly one;
The conscious and the unconscious,
both are His footstools.
He is neither manifest nor hidden,
He is neither revealed nor unrevealed.
There are no words to tell that which He is.

Kabir, a 15th Century East Indian mystic
(Tagore 2002, p 52-53)

No tongue can tell Your secret
for the measure of the word
Obscures Your nature.

But the gift of the ear
is that it hears
what the tongue
cannot tell.

Hakim Sanai, 12th Century Persian poet.
(Hemenway, 2002, p. 77)

The way to You
lies clearly in my heart,
and cannot be seen
or known
to the mind.
As my words
turn to
silence,
Your sweetness
surrounds me.

Hakim Sanai
(ibid p. 38)

Out beyond ideas of wrongdoing and rightdoing
there is a field.
I'll meet you there.

When the soul lies down in that grass,
the world is too full to speak;
Ideas, language, even the phrase each other
Doesn't make any sense.

Rumi, 16th Century Islamic Sufi
(Barks, 1997, 36)

The sum of all perfection is
To be always loving the Beloved.

St. John of the Cross – 16th Century Christian mystic

In the Beginning

I, Wisdom, call out to all to search for me. I laid the foundations of the world. Those who seek Me with their whole heart find me. To capture my Essence with your mind is like trying to hold flames of fire in your hand. To embrace me with your heart is to be enflamed with Truth. Hildegard of Bingen, who lived in the Rhine Valley in the 12th Century, loved Me well. She was graced with many visions which were recorded and painted, so that future generations would benefit from her insights. In one vision she saw the Universe as an egg and I, Wisdom spoke clearly to her.

"I, the highest and fiery power have kindled every spark of life and emit nothing that is deadly. I decide on all reality. With wisdom I have rightly put the Universe in order. With my lofty wings I fly above the globe. I, the fiery life of Divine essence am aflame beyond the beauty of the meadows; I gleam in the waters; I burn in the sun, moon and stars. With every breeze, as with invisible life that contains everything, I awaken everything to life."

Yes, I awaken everything to life, and I am here to awaken you to who you really are. As I begin your story, I want you to embrace one truth — the truth of story. There have always been many creation stories. Many of these stories have been lost in modernity. In ancient times, people would sit around a fire and the elders would tell story after story about all the wonders and lessons of life, stories about the history of their tribe, and many stories of how the world began. Creation stories were never one single story and were never taken literally, for the elders knew that the world of Mystery could only be embraced in myth, archetypes, ritual, symbol and story. Stories are meant to capture the imagination and fill souls with wonder and awe, where my wisdom lives and the Beloved rests. Yes the awe of the One is the beginning of wisdom. Awe and wonder are the first signs that my wisdom is at work. And awe does not divide but brings souls together in celebration of Mystery.

One of the first creation stories actually written down was in the book of Job. Job is an archetype of all humanity. Job suffered every affliction imaginable and everyone suffers one, or some, of these afflictions in life. He remained faithful and praised God declaring the manifold wisdom of God in all of creation. The response of the Beloved was not validation, but a challenge, "Where were you when I laid the foundation of the earth? Have you ever commanded a morning?" Over and over again, Job was questioned about how to make lightning, or snow, or streams. Of course, Job admitted that he was not there in the beginning, did not know how creation came forth, and most certainly could not create land, or sea, or creature. In this great exercise in humility, Job was transformed into a mystic, and the mystic embraced Mystery. And so too I, Holy Wisdom, say to all of you: Were you there? Can you make the snow to fall, or hang a rainbow in the sky? Were any of your holy prophets there in the beginning? My friends, it is foolish to argue over what you cannot make. Is it not enough to be grateful for the Beauty of it all? It is and will always be a Mystery. All the scientific research available to you now must make you marvel all the more! You have pictures of other galaxies! You know that there are more than 100 billion galaxies. Be in awe! Be amazed! But don't be stubborn. The Universe is One. Everything is One. There is no divorce in Essence; you can not divide Essence anymore than you can slice the air. To take the spiritual out of creation would be to live without breathing. Science, spirituality, and all matters of intelligence, are tools for

In The Beginning

the quest; they are only different avenues of exploration. Embrace the unity, and you will come to Unity. And the best way to flow in unity is to see the story. Are you ready? Possibly pour yourself your favourite drink, and snuggle into a comfortable chair. Remember, the story is true, and maybe it actually happened.

Imagine then, we are leaving this galaxy, passing the planets, passing Jupiter, the big brother planet that shields and protects Earth. We pass through hundreds, thousands, millions, and then billions of galaxies. The clock has rolled back almost fourteen billion years. Try to imagine - no time and no space.

Once upon a no-time, the Universe was everywhere, and as tiny as a …. this I will tell you later. In this no-time, no-space, the Beloved was, and is, and always will be. Now, I will use the past tense, but in the Beloved, there are no tenses. Every moment is this moment. So, the Beloved was alone and oh how She dreamed. She longed to express all of her inner Beauty and Intelligence. She wanted to know and be known. She dreamed of relating, relationships, connections, interconnections, community, expressing her love, and being loved in return, and all things loving each other. She wanted to display her vastness, her wonder, and intricate beauty. She literally ached to experience Herself in dimensions not yet created. She longed for millions of beings all flowing in love. Then that wasn't enough. Her dream grew and grew. Still she was filled with longing unexpressed. She continued to dream. She imagined a vast expanse of harmony, of planets orbiting, stars and creatures, tiny little legs making webs and great cosmic webs spanning entire galaxies; everything so intricately connected. Oh, how her heart was bursting with desire to touch, to feel, to experience her Sacred Unity expressed in all kinds of creations.

One moment, what actually became the first moment, as Beloved was in the deepest, meditative longing, a *tear* rolled down. She caught this tear and there! There, in this pool of primordial waters, She saw reflected all that She had longed for. Her entire dream was before her eyes. She was so overwhelmed. Very gently and reverently, She bent to kiss this tear, but I, the heat in her Holy Breath sent this tear off – and the Universe was birthed with a kiss.

I, Hokhmah, swirled in ecstatic motion, and, for the first *time*, I began to feel the heat of my Essence, many degrees hotter than your Sun. It was electric and magnetic. Binah, Spirit of Intelligent Beauty, was there in the cool waters pregnant with infinite, intimate possibilities. As she drew away from me, such a tease, elements cooled, and particles formed. What miracles exploded and flared forth in seconds. We continued our dance, lost in a whirlwind of delight, and from these first elements, galactic clouds formed. We were full of ecstasy and bliss! Oh how we danced, Intelligent Beauty; Holy Breath, and I. We had star dust fights. The clouds danced in us and we danced in them. We were the experience, and the witness; as within, so without. Bursting with exploding passion, a Mystery was unfolding. New dimensions of time and space made for endless possibilities now. We were filled with anticipation of what was yet to come.

The magic and beauty of the Invisible realm was being clothed with elements: invisible heaven and visible heaven, all one beautiful reality. All that was in the dream of the Beloved was becoming visible; a great marriage of intelligence. Your scientists today say that they can investigate visible matter after a few seconds of this flaring forth; they know something happened to begin the Universe almost 14 billion years ago. Little did they know or even consider that it was a kiss! That tiny, yet vast Universe was all in the tear!

Well, it took us a billion years to form galaxies. Things were intense, dark, and chaotic. Stars were born and died. Within the womb of larger stars called supernovas, we created the elements of life. The gift of sacrifice is crucial in this story. When stars die, they release carbon, without which you could not be.

Ten billion years we were at work, in darkness, in chaos, exploding, colliding, dying and birthing. Those are stories for others to hear. It was after ten billion years that a crucial moment took place for you. A wonderful grandmother star became a supernova and gave up her life in an explosion that gave rise to Earth's life-sustaining one, the Sun. Still dizzy with delight, from the Sun we spun this Solar System like a necklace adorned for a queen.

Comets and meteorites pelted Earth's thickening crust as it cooled off. The Moon was born. Over hundreds of millions of years, Earth had grown from dust particles to a large, hot, molten planet with a thin rocky crust. My fiery Essence was fast at work in the burning heat of the volcanoes, trembling and shaking with anticipation. Binah, Spirit of Intelligent Beauty, rose in the steam, and gathered her greatest gift – water. As the steam condensed above the Earth, there were the miracles of rain and weather systems. The first rains fell, and then torrential rains fell until rivers ran over the land and pooled into great seas.

Four billion years ago Intelligent Beauty and I began to really feel like parents. Small creatures called bacteria were born; it was our first living cell.

After a few million years, these bacteria ran out of free food supplies. Ingeniously we watched, from within and without, our little first-borns at work. They did it! They invented ways to capture energy from the Sun for new sources of food from water and simple minerals. But, in the process of eating these new forms of food, they gave off oxygen. For them, this was a deadly corrosive gas that eventually piled up in the atmosphere and threatened all of life. We became almost paralyzed with grief! We had come so far. Over ten billion years, something I know you can't comprehend, and at last life! Now it seemed that all could be gone. For another two billion years we waited in patience, and trust. We just kept on believing in the vision. The Beloved remembered again and again her dream in that tear. Binah and I knew our wisdom and understanding were silently at work somehow.

Well, then it happened! All kinds of oxygen-loving grandchildren emerged. It was a proud time! Life was growing and expanding. These bacteria formed little cooperatives and willingly gave up their independence for the good of the whole community.

By one billion years ago, these creatures were eating each other for dinner, but it balanced and sustained itself.

Three hundred million years later, that is seven hundred million years ago, organisms began living together in colonies and communicating with each other with chemical messages.

Six hundred million years ago, we experienced the most fantastic miracle yet. Light sensitive eyespots evolved into eyesight and Earth saw herself for the first time! What celebration!

There is something miraculous about seeing, beholding the beauty all around. Inspiration abounds and creativity just blossoms. Soon there were soft-bodied animals and, over the next 70 million years, previously naked animals protected themselves with shells, jaws, beaks and skeletons. Millions of years went by, and then came the first plants and insects, and amphibians, the first to trade in their gills for lungs.

It was 460 million years ago that the oceans graciously and generously pushed up their grassy beds and lay on the Earth; from this the first forests were birthed. One hundred million years later, following the 4th and greatest mass extinction, dinosaurs, the first to be capable of loving, emerged. Subsequently, it took millions of years to make the first mammal, mammals demonstrating love, and then, about 150 million years later, birds graced the sky and flowers fragranced the land, arraying the Earth for the sweetest honeymoon. Sixty-five million years ago, Earth started greeting rodents, monkeys, whales, camels and all kinds of mammals.

We marveled at all of the beautiful, living creations flowing in harmony from that longing of long ago; every detailed part of the dream in the tear, and birthed from that kiss of loving intention. The Beloved was like the thread weaving all of creation into a tapestry of delight. I, Holy Wisdom and Intelligent Beauty wove the patterns. It was about 200,000 years ago that homo sapiens emerged, and by 50,000 years ago modern humans.

All that has come forth was in the Dream, in the tear, in the kiss. The Beloved's Breath, my Holy Fire, and Beauty's Womb of Water birthed all of Earth. We are always at work, within and without; it is all an unfolding Mystery. We were pleased to dwell in the sanctuary of Planet Earth.

This is Paradise: the Dream realized! I, Hokhmah, say to you, that I will never comprehend why so many humans think that Paradise is a realm you go to when you die. Where will you go, except to the ethereal realm of Love from which you came? There is no touch in that realm. There is no variety of species uniquely expressing their creation. This is Earth! This is the Dream! Heaven in Earth; Earth in Heaven – in the here and now – a miracle of miracles! Beloved has loved you before the foundations of the world. I was there, a great Witness to Her Dream, eager to show my delight in Her. We dreamed for so long and have worked so hard to experience you. You are a dream come true! You, just as you are - placed in this Paradise of Pleasure, this Garden of Desire. Witness the vast beauty all around? Could you dream of anything more wonderful? This is the Mystery revealed and unrevealed - Heaven in Earth; Earth in Heaven. You are living the dream; there is no greater bliss than to be a person fully alive and awake. All that you see is Heaven manifest. It is our Dream! It is our Delight! It is for the Pleasure of all living beings, creatures, forests and waters. It is Life manifest.

Find anything in Nature that you find beautiful and study it until you realize that that is you; you are that. You are the dancing brook, the blooming lotus, and the wind that rustles in the trees. Know that everything you witness is you. All is one. If you seem to be lacking a quality, find it in Nature and embrace its uniqueness. If you lack strength, go to the rocks or the mountains and listen. If you feel stuck, study a stream. Let the winged ones, and all the creatures, be your teachers. They have much to show you. Experience the serenity of the forests, and the splendour of all Earth. Fall in love with everything, because everything has always been in love with you.

Take time for reflection in the Beauty of Nature.

Thank-you

Thank-you my Love
If you didn't take on human form,
I couldn't kiss You.
If you didn't manifest in creation,
I couldn't see You.
If you didn't make the brook to run,
I couldn't hear You.
Ahh, your Beauty!
You've gone to so much effort,
to show me
You.

April, 2005

Keepers of the Sacred Tear

*T*he uniqueness of the human species is they were the ones who agreed to be the basins of the Sacred Tear. Everything in Creation is a reflection of her invisible Beauty and Wonder. None of this would have come to be, if She did not first Dream. So She needed to find a species willing to reflect her as Dream, a creature that would be willing to be a witness to her Longing. The Beloved wanted to have her longing returned to Her; She wanted to be the dream, someone's dream. You took on this task. Out of your tremendous love for Her, for everything, you agreed, in your primordial consciousness, to hold the tear. It is the greatest gift of all; and, as is so often the case, it is the heaviest to bear. Life becomes a quest. The human journey is a longing to find Her, a search for Truth.

So the human is birthed in forgetfulness, for how can one long for what one has? You forget who you really are. You forget the Beloved. There is the deep call in your heart to seek. You yearn to know the Beloved. You are compelled to find out who you really are, to search for Truth, and to express your inner passion. It is a journey. You give the greatest gift to the Beloved, in the searching, in your seeking. But you were never meant to be so ill equipped for this journey. You need sound teachers and wise elders who have reached their quest. You need communities established in love to hold you, because the abyss of darkness is fearful, and the yearning of not knowing can be ache. That is why I am speaking so clearly to you. That is why I'm telling you this story — to help you on your journey.

So, it is you, precious human, who can dream, first and foremost to know the Beloved again; and then to realize your own inner dreams of creativity. If you can dream it, you can do it; the power is in the dream. Just like the Beloved, if it is something you long to do, a beauty you long to create, you can. Every time you love, you create; when you make peace, you create; when you heal or bring joy, you are living your creative beauty. Anything and everything you bring forth from your imagination, be it a meal for a friend, a room decorated, an innovative way of teaching, and on and on, is all from your sacred tear. As you create, you are the most precious imitator of your Beloved. Live your dreams and live them well!

Reflection: What is it that you long to do? Love that longing. Hold it. Picture it and give it a kiss.

There is a basic principle for welcoming evolution
as not denigrating the work of God
But actually revealing a more intimate presence
in cosmic history than we had dreamed possible.

Matthew Fox
(Fox 1985, 44)

The Universe
Is
A community of subjects
Not
A collection of objects.

Thomas Berry

Tear Drop

A tear drop hangs expectantly
at the tip of the pine needle's entry to eternity
enfolding the tenses of being
in its fluid clarity,
crept silently from the eye of divinity
flowed down the long expanse
of smooth needle cheek.
I bathe in its nutrient wetness
I curl up in its perfect truth
I gasp expectantly in its possibility
languishing just this side of gravity
preparing for evaporation
preparing to escape
its needle-informed form.
We yearn,
it and I
for our destiny;

In The Beginning

will it drop
will I see it
does it contain all that is
is it just the beginning
of all that might be? The scent of pine
the hint of breezy breath
and the cry of a jay
cascade through my senses
inviting me to the mystery...
offering no easy answers...
stirring me
to smile with gratitude
for this moment,
for this blessing
of liquid wakefulness.

(Note: 82406
Written while sitting in one of the Muskoka chairs on the hill overlooking the pond at the front of the property we call Cairncrest, while reflecting on the heavy dew that filled the morning walk with Maya. Influenced by a story of the creation of Universe by Nancy Cleaves.)

Jake McArthur

Keepers of the Sacred Tear – Listen

I am Hokhmah, Holy Wisdom, and I thank you for listening. It is my call to awaken you to who you really are: keepers of the Sacred Tear. In the tear you see the reflection of your Beloved, the entire Universe and the beauty of your wondrous souls. Giving loving attention to your tear, your longings, will enable you to bring forth the creative beauty to restore this loving planet Earth and its species. You know that all of Earth is in deep agony at this time. It took so long to create, and so quickly is She killed. I, Hokhmah, am in so much pain. All of creation groans and travails waiting for you to fully wake up to your true selves and true calling; living in your truth empowers you to stop those who destroy. You are people of compassion. When someone is in pain, the greatest gift is a compassionate ear. The gift of listening doesn't change the present circumstances, but changes everything that really matters: the inner realm of soul. Compassion heals and brings hope for the future. You see, it is I who cries. I am the One who needs a compassionate ear. I am everywhere. My Voice is upon the waters; my yearnings beneath your feet. As it is recorded in the book of Thomas, "Split a piece of wood and you will find me; turn over a stone, and I am there." So I thank you now for listening to my pain.

Mother Earth

"I am Mother Earth. I flow with the Mystery of Divine Compassion. My heart beats with the rhythm of Sacred Unity. It took billions and billions of years to make my form and then many more to beautify me with oils and fragrances. I have been crowned with jewels and clothed in lushness. When I came of age I gave birth to the finest of living swimming, crawling, flying and walking species.

For thousands and thousands of years I have been honoured and revered. I told my Story over and over again. The trees sang it back to me. The oceans roared with laughter at the miracle of it all. Quiet streams caressed me with soothing echoes of delight. Life! Over and over again, tiny and great miracles of Life were birthed, each Living creature heralding the Maker of All and adoring Me for
my fertility.

I've endured catastrophes of great magnitude, tempest storms and blight, but with each hardship I learned and have grown stronger and wiser. I remember the delight of birthing the human, the people of the sacred tear, the one species chosen to give back to the Great Creator the gift that has birthed the entire Universe, longing and birthing intimate intention.

These chosen ones have become my horror. They are destroying everything and torturing Me, yes Me, their own Mother. I have watched so many of my dear little Ones die off or be killed, entire species that are no more. Day after day these humans batter Me with bombs and blasts. I have shattered fragments and gaping wounds. They have stolen my oils and my skin is now dry and withering. And moment after moment, they – rape Me. They cut down my lush robe and I am laid bare and helpless.

I have almost nowhere to bathe for the waters are becoming stench. Once I breathed in the deep blue sky and now He too is old and gray, suffocating, like Me. Alas these humans are caging me in cement. This must be my coffin. I guess this is the end …

unless…

the keepers of the sacred tear listen."

Living Water Speaks

"Keepers of the sacred tear:

You see Me clearly, don't you?
You love everything about Me;
I'm pure, refreshing,
So clean, no secrets.

I reflect the Beauty of the Above
To the Earth below,
So that you may know
All is One.
Physical expresses the Invisible.
I reflect the Physical.
It's all One Reality.

But you're changing that.
How will you see once I am nothing but murk?
How will you be cleansed in blackened streams?
How will you be refreshed in stench-filled ravines?

> You lose Me,
> You lose You.
> We are One;
> Only One Reality.

> You kill Me,
> You kill You.

> Hear my cry
> In every ripple.

Hear my wail
On every shore.

Feel my heart reaching out
With every wave.

Don't kill Me!
Please! No more!

Keepers of the sacred tear, listen."

The Trees Rock the Cradle in Protest

"We are the home of medicinal healing remedies.
We are the haven of delicate species.
We are the filter of human breath.
Our roots go deep anchoring soil.
We maintain the balance of wetness
and dryness of Earth.

You cut us down for more land to graze animals
To stuff your mouths or fill urban sprawls.
You burn us at the stake
As if heretics to your faith.
Indeed!
You take our finest for your empty houses
Bigger, More, Finer.
For what?

For millions of years we have stood
Tall
Anchoring your souls to Mother;
Rooting your consciousness to the
Sacredness and Oneness of All that
Springs from Her Grace.
We have sheltered you from heat, wind and cold
And wrapped our healing leaves
To make you whole.
For what?

*We have grown bitter.
We have watched too much death.
Cut us down! Cut us all!
We wish to see no more.
Rain forests, you can finally
cease your cries
For you will be – no more.*

*We loved you with our greenness,
Our lushness,
Our warmth, our healing hearths;
We sacrificed willingly for you
As people would gather around
Our burning souls,
And stories tell
And sing and dance.
We were glad then. It was very well.*

Now
We're tired.
Our boughs are breaking
For the heaviness we carry;
We have cradled
A selfish, destructive people
For too long.
For what?"

Wind's Breath

"I am the Mysterious One;
You feel but can't touch;
You know but can't see.
In Me, you breathe.

I am the Connector
To all Living
Ever flowing, moving
In Me, you are One.

I am Life
Invigorating, Expanding,
Revitalizing Energy.
In Me, you live.

Now,
I am suffocating
With gases unknown,
Poisons and pollutants clog my throat.
In you, I die.

Keepers of the sacred tear, listen."

Earth's Carpet

A sea of cement,
Concrete and cold,
Tells us no stories
Of Nature of old.
Robbed and broken
The grass beneath
Whispers its cries
Underneath the creeks.

"How are your feet?
I miss your soles.
How I loved to brush
And tickle your toes.
You thought
Nothing
Removing my tender blades;
But
Now that I'm gone,
Was it a fair exchange?"

Keepers of the sacred tear – listen.

Voice of the Ancients

"We are the ancestors: those who honoured the spiritual path, walked in mutual respect with all living creatures; we are the keepers of the sacred circle which has been broken by the self-serving generations. Millions of our people have been killed and our culture stolen. Yet, we are peacemakers and hold sacred space for you to return to your tribal teachings and join our circle again. Only together can we heal Mother Earth and living species."

Listen
Or
Thy Tongue
Will Make Thee
Deaf

Native Proverb

The Divine Human

I, Holy Wisdom, am the sap of the Universe. From the beginning of beginnings I am with my Beloved. I want to tell the story of your beginnings. You have many names and no name, and many stories of your creation, but I choose one story that you are familiar with, the story of *Adam*, both male and female. In ancient Hebrew Adam is spelled with letter aleph, one of the three mother letters, 'ah', like the sound one makes at the sight of a newborn. The next three letters spell 'dam' which means blood, juice, wine, sap, or essence. So, Adam is a being birthed with delight from the Beloved and flows with the sap of the Universe.

Beloved said, "I will take the firmest rocks from the mountains and fashion a skeleton; this will be their structure so that they will know that they are beings of 'faith', 'rooted confidence'; nothing is impossible to them and their existence is as sure and as mighty as the mountains. Then I will wrap them in *adamah*, Earth so that they will never forget their connection to sacred *Earth* and to all that grows and is sustained by her goodness. I will place one of my Holy Sparks deep within them that can never be extinguished but can be enflamed to light up their true essence. Then I will breathe in them my 'Holy Breath'. I will give them two cavities so that they can breathe deeply and be filled with my Essence. These cavities will be called lungs and placed equally in both sides of their beings and in this they will remember the importance of equality between left and right, feminine and masculine, yin and yang. I will make it that they have to inhale and exhale regularly; with every breath they may realize that 'hayye' (life) is ever flowing, receiving and giving, and never attaching. At the core of all life, is light, wave and particle; the dance of love around the silence of stillness."

After the Holy One was finished speaking, I, Hokhmah, Holy Wisdom, turned very serenely and said, "I know what I must contribute. I will provide the 'dam' in 'Adam', the 'blood, essence, juice, sap, wine'. I will take some of our Holy Fire, let it cool and then cause it to flow throughout their entire being. When they breathe in holy breath, breath will be mixed with 'dam', giving all the nutrients necessary to all the cells of their body. This sap will not only provide nutrition but will heal wounded parts and circulate continually bringing growth and vitality. I will gather this essence of my wine, shape it into a heart and put it into the core of their being, a little to the left which is controlled by the right brain of intuition and creativity; in this they will know that balance to the rational left brain comes from embracing fully the virtues of the right brain. I will fill the essence of 'dam' with love so they will come back into the awareness that You, Holy One, are Love; life experience is all about Love. But this heart will be broken as well as filled with blissful devotion. Those who do not choose love will bring harm to others and their blood will flow in pain and suffering as well as healing. I will be their blood, Beloved, and I will dwell with and among them and show them that I am the One who suffers with them; I will carry their pain and bring them to renewed life and wholeness."

Beloved turned tenderly towards Me, and with searching eyes She lovingly embraced Me. As in all holy moments, there was no exchange of words. Our eyes said it all. The Beloved One knew I was choosing to suffer as I bore the essence of humanity in my fiery Life. I will never forget this moment. Both adoration and sadness were in her eyes. In the most affectionate embrace She gently kissed my height, then my depth, my width, and my breadth. Warm tears caressed me. Then I felt such a tender and affectionate kiss on my heart, the centre of my Being. She forever sealed me with these kisses. She crossed my Essence in the four directions, showing that as these beloveds endure the pain of betrayal and loss by giving forgiveness and showing mercy, their compassion will extend far out into the four directions. Then I said, "Beloved, I want their hearts to beat, moment by moment with the rhythm of the Universe. With every beat, may they be drawn closer to the remembrance of Me."

The Holy Spirit of Binah was sitting engagingly and ponderingly by. "I want to fill their beings with the Water of Life. I will be the amniotic fluid that nurtures, protects and brings forth at the right moment. I don't want to beat, nor be inhaled and exhaled; I want to be silent and still so that as they remember to be still; in Me they will see the reflection of the Beauty of the entire Universe within them. I want to mirror all of creation for them in my still Waters. I want to reflect You, Holy Beloved, in the silence of their souls"

Just as we were ready to make the first Adam, I saw that deep longing look in my Beloved's eyes. What is it? "This is the one who will hold my tear. They will love Me in their longings."

And so the human, keeper of the sacred tear, was formed, first as one, and then as two, so that the human will always work to be in balance with the masculine and feminine, yin and yang, in their own souls. The human was placed in the lush forests, cascading water falls, and austere mountains with all manner of beautiful species. There, in the sanctuary of planet Earth, the Beloved rested and in the tabernacle of the human soul, this tear of intimate longing found its home.

All the mysteries of the Universe and all of my Holy Wisdom were hidden in the high collective conscience, the nashama. It cannot be tarnished nor extinguished. Those who search deep into their souls are also raised high in their illumination and celebration of consciousness. The invitation is always there for each person, to awaken to their divine essence, and enjoy sweet intimacy with the Beloved and All Life. The Beloved marveled at your intelligence as you recognized the unique beauty in all creatures, and your loving care towards them. Many answered the call of intimacy and communion, and many did not.

With every birth of everything, Beloved is like a new Mother over and over. There is no end to her joy. And so it is for you. With the birthing of every infant, She is overwhelmed with tender affection. Everyone is so unique, and so special. No one is like you. She celebrates you just as you are. I will speak much more about your childhoods later when I tell the story of the Universe as your cosmic journey. At this moment, my heart is moved deeply to communicate one truth from the heart of the Beloved. There is only One Essence – Love. You are birthed from Love, in Love, and for Love. Your beauty is innate; your goodness inherent. You embody divinity. Your essence is a sacred melody orchestrating Heaven in Earth and Earth in Heaven.

So many of you have been told that you are not worthy as you are; that you are sentenced to an eternity in hell and damnation. Beloved is crushed. You could not bear to hear Her wailing in grief for her beloved, cherished children. So many sons and daughters for countless centuries never come close to discovering their true essence. Instead of a quest made in love, it is a quest to find love. Instead of a journey to discover one's true potential, it is a journey to discover any sense of self worth. The burdens, the guilt and the fear that this teaching brings is almost too much to bear. I will let the Beloved say how She feels in her own words.

*I didn't know
I would cause you such pain.
My heart aches
again and again.*

*My dear beloveds,
fruit of my soul,
living with no hope,
no quest for the whole.*

*False teaching
has broken your heart and mine;
Made you feel worthless,
no sense of divine.*

*Let me hold you
as a babe to my breast.
Trust me and listen,
I will bring you to rest.*

*It's time for mending
what's broken and lost.
For you, I will do anything,
no great, the cost.*

*Can you believe Me?
Trust Me to Be?
I am what I am,
Only Love for thee.*

*From My heart to yours,
Your Beloved*

If you listen, you can hear Her calling you in every moment, as you breathe in each breath. She never stops. She can't. She is Love and waits for love to return to Her.

Reflection: Practice being loving and gentle with yourself. Reflect often on your true essence. Journal your reflections. Know that whatever you love about the Beloved is also what you love about yourself. You are Her mirror.

From Before the Before

Holy One, I see the Land to which you are calling me:
A place where I will know touch, taste, fragrance,
sight and sound
in unfolding Beauty.
It entices me, calls me, brings forth a deep yearning.
I will not know myself unless I am birthed in this
Land,
I know.
And I know – First, I must die.
I'm scared.
Will I forget You? Will I forget me?
Here I am safe and protected,
Yet so limited in my ethereal existence.
Here I know only Light.
What will the darkness be like?
How will I find You – again?

Little one, precious,
Remember,
When you feel the Wind,
Hear Water,
Sit by Fire,
I AM there.
When you lie on Earth,
You are there.
Marry us.
This is Life;
This is Being.

(Sept., 2005)

In the Awe

Think of the beauty
In all that you are;
Realize the wonder
Live in the awe.

From Beauty you came forth;
Beauty you are.
Wonder is your birth.
Live in the awe.

Wisdom is your life.
Counsel your fine clothes.
Radiance is your crown.
Love your fine robe.

From Beauty you came forth;
Beauty you are.
Wonder is your birth.
Live in the awe.

Surety is your steps.
Delight is your dance.
Fragrance upon your lips;
Heaven and Earth's Romance.

From Beauty you came forth;
Beauty you are.
Wonder is your birth.
Live in the awe.

The Divine Human

The stars are your eyes,
Deep Darkness your cape,
Witnessing the splendour,
Of Mystery's wake.

From Beauty you came forth;
Beauty you are.
Wonder is your birth.
Live in the awe.

(Thanksgiving 2009)

When I think

Of

The Beloved,

I am in Awe,

Motionless.

When I think

Of

The Beloved in me,

I dream,

Boundless.

(Oct. 1999)

The breeze at dawn has secrets to tell you.
Don't go back to sleep.

You must ask for what you really want.
Don't go back to sleep.

People are going back and forth
across the doorsill, where the two worlds touch.
The door is round and open.
Don't go back to sleep

Rumi
(Barks 1997, 36)

The Witness of Abraham

*R*emember, my friends, above all, this is one story. One Divine Beloved, one Wisdom, one Beauty, one Creation – a Cathedral of Celebration, one Human – a Sacred Tabernacle, and all from One Tear of Longing Expression. It is One River of Life which flows with the Current of Love, for all and in all. There is One Holy Breath that gives Life to all. I, Hokhmah, always send forth sages, prophets, teachers and guides, to help you find your way Home, deep within your Sacred Souls. There, is the Living Reflection of all that is – Love and Beauty. If you look for the story, my wisdom can shine and enlighten your path. There are many precious souls, who do seek Me, but can't find Me; they miss the story because they have been taught literal views.

I'm referring to the fundamental stream of the three religions birthed from the ecology of the Middle East. Fundamental beliefs breed arrogance and intolerance. Each group claims to have God all figured out and every one else is wrong. I, Wisdom, call to all those with these views. To be devoted to the Beloved is good, but She is bigger and greater than all the religions of the world combined. One hundred billion galaxies can not define Her. You are participants in making Her Dream on this planet come true, and Her Dream is for all beings, all creatures, and all creation to flow in love, harmony, and beauty. There is no division in love.

You all claim Abraham as your leader. Through Abraham, in Abraham, before Abraham, I Am. My wisdom expressed in Abraham is about *surrender*. This is the meaning of the word 'Islam'. Surrender is the primary call to all humans; surrender initiates one on his or her journey. Abraham left his home town, left all that was familiar, and followed Beloved's call. It is not a story to be taken literally, that the people in the town of Ur were unworthy, or their form of worship was false. No, Abraham left and started a new journey. This story teaches you, that this soul journey is a sole journey. One must search for the Beloved in one's own heart; the quest for truth is an individual quest. Maybe you have a loving, and a very devotional community; but the community can not give you an inner experience of the Beloved. They can guide, help, teach, and encourage you. But it is your intention, your heart motivation that matters. Like Abraham, you follow Beloved's call in your own heart and journey with that call.

So, Abraham left. As much as there is a lot to gain from his entire story, I want to focus on *surrender*. Abraham was promised a son, and was given Isaac at a very old age. Sarah laughed thinking she was too old to give birth. So then, here is the wisdom, you are never too old for any promise, or to live as a blessing.

Beloved gave Abraham a profound test in this area of surrender. Would he be willing to release Isaac? Abraham passed the test and offered Isaac, not in sacrifice, but in surrender. This spiritual journey is one of complete surrender to all attachments. The wonderful blessings, and gifts of family and friendship, are not possessions, or people you can control; just as Isaac was not Abraham's possession. Power for this long journey starts and ends in letting go – surrender – time and time again. Abraham's long awaited blessing had to be surrendered. All you have is the Beloved. Even the blessings that come your way are nothing to claim as your own.

As happens often enough, Abraham thought the Beloved needed a little help in fulfilling the promise of a son, and Hagar gave birth to Ishmael. When Isaac came along, Abraham banished Hagar and his son Ishmael. Abraham was a human being, influenced by the customs and norms of the day. I, Hokhmah, am often not heard because my Wisdom has not entered into the consciousness of the people. This is true of patriarchy. In the patriarchal beliefs of the day, only the oldest son inherited the blessing. Beloved abounds with love, and blessings could have been extended to both sons, but patriarchal thinking hindered this flow of love. My wisdom and advice were unheard. Abraham banished his own son, punished Hagar, who had obeyed him, and sent them forsaken, abandoned, and to die alone. But Beloved heard their cries.

My wisdom is about balance. Any one person who lives by patriarchal thinking could be likened to an airplane. One wing is tipped high in the sky – masculine honour; and the other wing is tipped to the ground – feminine dishonour. The plane is doomed to crash. When you honour the feminine and masculine equally, the plane flies smoothly; there is balance and wholeness. Whether it is the oldest son honoured over the younger, or men honoured over women, patriarchy divides, oppresses, shames, and enslaves souls, mostly women, to a life of heartache. My dearest friends, this should not be so.

Masculine energy alone is harsh, domineering, and leads to cruelty and violence; but balanced with the feminine, it is strong and protective; and leads to compassion and harmony. The global community is in peril from testosterone overload. Almost all cultures have been gravely affected by patriarchy. Men, every time you give honour and respect to a woman, you give it to yourself. You too, are in need of being gentle with yourselves. As you release patriarchal views, your daughters will be blessed with the kindness and gentleness that they deserve. Honour them in every way. Teach your sons to respect women. Show them to respond in grace to their own feelings; so many are hardened at a young age, thinking it is a shame to cry. They feel isolated, confused, and very lonely.

On the worst extreme, their locked up emotions turn to anger and rage, and, as William Pollock stated, 'boys cry bullets'.

I am Hokhmah, and before you I have set a table. It is a banquet table, and full of abundance. The celebration is the greatest wedding of all time; it is the marriage of the masculine and the feminine. It is a union of mutual love and respect for the unique qualities that each has, both within each of you and in each gender. This union must take place first in your own attitude toward the Beloved (masculine, feminine, and other), then in your own soul; in small communities, and then in the culture at large. This is no small task. I, Wisdom, have been trying to illuminate your consciousness in love and honour toward the Divine Feminine for a long time. When Shekhinah is respected, the Messiah will rise up. Shekhinah is the Feminine Presence of Beloved, banished until humanity learns to live in love and harmony. Messiah is the fully awakened human soul who lives in prophetic insight. The joy, the bliss that awaits this marriage, is beyond your fondest dreams: it is nothing less than *malkutah*: Heaven on Earth.

So, to my Muslim friends, and to my Jewish friends, it is time for Isaac and Ishmael to come together to the Table of Abundance. It is time for Hagar to be honoured and come Home. And it is time for absolutely everyone to come to the Marriage Feast!

Abraham was right and good in his generosity. When he came to the promised land, he asked Lot where he wanted to live. Lot chose the best land. My Jewish friends, are you really of Abraham? Ask the Palestinians where they want to live. There is room for all when you realize the only Promised Land is the landscape of your soul, and everywhere a foot walks is sacred soil.

To my Christian friends, do you really expect your messiah to come to bless you and kill everyone else? In the Life of the Beloved all live. In the Breath, all breathe.

If you put a true Christian, who lives as Yeshua lived, beside a true Muslim, who lives the Quran, beside a true Jew, who lives the

Torah, all would look the same. Laying aside religious clothing, you would not recognize one from the other for they are all loving people. They love the Beloved with all of their hearts, and this is all that matters. They try to live in peace and kindness toward all.

It's time to put on your wedding gown, all of you, everyone. The invitation has long been given. I will dress you in the finest robes, and adorn you with the finest jewels. Abundance and celebration awaits you. All you have to do is follow the spirit of Abraham and surrender; surrender to your journey as he did, surrender all attachments, and surrender to something he couldn't - to love of the Divine Feminine.

Reflection: Talk to people from different spiritual traditions and visit their places of worship. Observe and ask questions. Look for the unity of heart.

Patriarchy does not die easily. Try to regard the Beloved in Feminine terms. Men, listen to the women in your life; listen to their perspectives, opinions and feelings on all matters that are important to you. Try to embrace life through their eyes.

Daily, ask the Beloved to soften your heart towards women, and to open your eyes to the fullness of your own being: masculine and feminine.

Hold on or Flow

You want to hold on
to something – someone.
This is mine you say.
This person has to love me;
They belong to me.

Hold on then – and
Hold onto your breath.
How long can you claim
Mine?
Hold onto your breath.
It's panic in your body;
Cells cut off from life-giving oxygen,
Stifling, stagnant,
stealing all your might,
as you hold your breath in fright.

Ahh – so you let it go.
Yes, you must.
Let it go! Let him go! Let her go!
Everything – everyone
is but a breath.
If you get to breathe them,
It is a gift.
Moment after moment,
Breath after breath,
Everything; Everyone; Every moment;
A gift.
Nothing to claim,
No-one to own,
Just breathing,
Receiving – Giving in the flow.

(March, 2009)

I am called

to be a loving parent

to my awkward,

and disturbing qualities,

And let them know that my soul

is a home

where there is

No judgement,

or febrile hunger

for a fixed and limited identity.

(Source Unknown)

The Witness of Moses

*E*very myth, every archetype, and story is part of the one story. Abraham's story gives valuable insights for all people. Moses, in particular, has a lot of my wisdom to give to this generation. As you know, Moses was rescued as a baby, and grew up in Pharaoh's court. He had access to all the power and priviledge anyone could want. When he discovered that he was really of the tribe of Israel, and it was his tribe being oppressed, he made an honourable choice. He resisted the temptation that wealth offers, and chose compassion for his people. Here is the test that comes to everyone, whether there is individual access to wealth or not: love of money, or love for love's sake.

When Moses took his calling literally, he picked up a sword and slew the Egyptian. Then he had to run for his own life. Violence begets violence – always. Oppression and injustice are everywhere. But the minute the oppressed kill, they have become the oppressor, and the vicious cycle continues. Even if you don't actually pull the trigger, if your theology involves killing others, it is, as Karen Armstrong writes, a 'militant piety'. The attitude of your heart supplies the ammunition. My friends, the Beloved's love for all does not fit in fundamental views that give one group redemption and everyone else damnation. Love includes everyone; this story is for all. I can restore your hope for peace and harmony attained through love, not through violence. In truth, the only real enemy is that which lies within one's own heart. Oppressed and oppressor have both been enslaved to a false sense of being: one believes he or she has the power to oppress and the other, that he or she has no power to stop being oppressed. Let's follow Moses. He found a way to end oppression – a much better way.

Moses put down his sword and retreated into the desert. It was there he found his true power. There, all is still and quiet. The landscape is bare; all can be revealed. There are no distractions. It is in the desert, that quiet and still place within your souls, that you find your true sense of being. The desert offers clarity of vision, discernment of what is true and not, and you realize there is no end to the landscape of your soul. The frontier is empty; you become empty. At a time when you least expect it, you hear the voice of the Beloved enflaming you with spiritual courage. You will rise up empowered and fear not.

From this inner strength, you will stand up for the weak and oppressed, and those living species that have no voice. You have no need or desire to see another killing. Compassion rules your heart. Love rules all. There is no superior view, or right and wrong theology; you live in the power of spirit, the Source of life for everyone. Life is sacred, a gift. Moses led the whole tribe out of oppression, with no sword. One person of violence kills another or a few. One person of spiritual wisdom and love leads countless souls into the Truth that brings freedom.

As Moses stood on the banks of the Red Sea, it looked like an impossible impasse. Thousands of innocent people trusting his leadership standing with him, Pharaoh's army right behind them, and in front, a sea of water. That was the flow of Binah, always ready to give birth to new paths. The waters parted, and the people of Israel were led toward promised opportunities of abundance and grace, and it was not to any strength of man or weapons that brought them to this place, it was spiritual power. And the armies perished with their weapons.

Life in this 21st Century is at this impasse. Those who choose spiritual strength are passing over to new opportunities: to a life of peace, compassion and harmony for all people, and all of sacred Earth. Those who choose violence, and the violence from greed, bring their own downfall and destruction.

Carl Jung said, 'Scratch a fundamentalist and you will find violence'. Fundamental views separate and categorize; there are the winners and the losers, no matter what arena the battle is fought in. Everyone lives by their perception. You are good-hearted people. I know your intention is not to hurt another. If you have fundamental views, you are being true to what you have been taught. Beloved sees your heart. I, Hokhmah, am your teacher. Binah, is with you as a guide and a comfort. Let's retreat into the desert of your soul together. It is a peaceful place. You can rest. There is a sacred fire of inspiration and empowerment waiting for you. It will make you a leader, beyond your dreams. Above all, you will *see* that you are a sacred being, and through those eyes, see that all of life is sacred; everyone is sacred. You will help many people to discover their inner Truth, and together create an Earth Home where it is safe for all Life.

Reflection: Are you intolerant of others for any reason? Spend time with them. Try to understand them. Look for the unity of heart.

Do you have seeds of violence in your thinking? Does your theology call for destruction of people or Earth? Ask Beloved to open your heart so that there is room for all creatures, all people from every walk of life, and all of creation. Give reverence to the one you think you oppose, and there you will find grace.

If you have been a victim of violence, in your grief, pray for peace. Your tears water the seeds.

Lovers of God

Lovers of God, sometimes a door opens,
and a human being becomes a way
for grace to come through.

I see various herbs in the kitchen garden, each with its own bed,
garlic, capers, saffron,
and basil, each watered differently to help it mature.

We keep the delicate ones separate from the turnips.
but there is room for all in this unseen world, so vast
that the Arabian Desert gets lost in it
Like a single hair in the ocean.

The Witness Of Moses

Imagine you are Sheba,
trying to decide whether to go to Solomon!
You're haggling about how much to pay for shoeing a
donkey,
when you could be seated with one
who is always in union with God,
who carries a beautiful garden inside himself.

You could be moving in a circuit without wing,
nourished without eating,
sovereign without a throne.
No longer subject to fortune,
you could be *luck* itself.

if you would rise from sleep, leave
the market arguing
and learn that your own essence is your wealth.

Rumi
(Barks 1995, 188, 189)

Yeshua, the Embodiment of Hokhmah

$\mathcal{N}$ow when Jesus, Yeshua, walked the Earth, many of his followers saw him as the embodiment of Me, Hokhmah, Holy Wisdom. Yes, my wisdom was so fully expressed in his life and teachings. To speak with any integrity of Yeshua, we must begin with his grandmother Anna and his mother Mary. Great sacrifices and great devotion prepared the way for Anna to become the soul she was and then to beget Mary. These women taught Yeshua the sacred path. To give honour to Yeshua is to revere these women and again turn attention to the grace of the Divine Feminine. Yeshua broke with cultural norms and took every opportunity to show equality and respect to the women in his day and had many devout disciples among them. I, Hokhmah, was diligently at work within Yeshua, trying to swing the pendulum away from patriarchy, to a place of balance and harmony. I am still fast at work, and the progress is far too slow. When the Divine Feminine is not honoured, everyone suffers. You need the gentle care and nurturing love of the Feminine to be restored.

Never was Yeshua more of a witness to the sacredness of your souls, as he was at his birth. Through this story, I was sending a clear call to all to come home to the innocence of your beginning. You come forth from the Beloved. You are treasured. You are Love in a body. When this child was born, the angels sang of peace on

Earth and goodwill to all. The angels sing that over every precious infant at birth. They bless you on your journey, that you find your inner peace, and as you do, that you will give divine goodness to all. This is your journey spoken simply: moment by moment come home to the realm of inner peace, and from this divine awareness, bring forth peace and goodness to all of life. The more you find the realm of harmony within, the more you bring it forth outwardly for all to enjoy. This is *malkutah*, heaven, within and without. Peace on Earth and goodwill to all is your birthright.

It was shepherds who came to honour Yeshua. Shepherd hearts, are people who live simply, know the seasons of life, and care for the animals. It is good for children to be surrounded by shepherd souls who will honour them and teach them the simple path of Truth. Then, the wise men came, men of great wealth in knowledge, bearing precious gifts. Look for the cosmologists in your life; the ones who are intrigued with the mysteries of the Universe. They are the ones who will expand your consciousness far beyond the stars. They will impart rare gifts to you.

Yeshua addressed women whenever he could, breaking with the social norms of the day. He honoured what was in a person's heart, and not any outward show, no matter what race one belonged to, or what creed one followed. He embraced the greatest instruction anyone, anywhere, in any time, could follow; he loved the Beloved with all of his heart. He did not worship himself – ever. To my Christian friends, your heart may be sincere, but you err to worship Yeshua. I am Hokhmah, the One who embodied him. I am from everlasting to everlasting, always in the Beginning. And even I do not require your worship. If you love Me, follow after Me; follow after Wisdom. If you follow Me, you will rule in this life through your heart of humility and grace, influencing many around you through your goodness. Yeshua prayed to the Beloved, not to himself. He said that if your eye is single, your whole body would be full of Light. If you focus on love, as he did, you will experience more and more illumination, and enlightenment, until it floods your entire being.

One of Yeshua's first teachings is called the 'Sermon on the Mount'. In his Native Aramaic language he started with this.

'Tubwayhun l'meskenaee b'rukh d'dilhounhie malkutah d'ashmaya.'
'Healed are those who devote themselves to the link of spirit;
The design of the universe is rendered through their form.'

or

'Blessed are those who know their only possession is in the Breath.'

The popular English translation is 'Blessed are the poor in spirit for theirs is the kingdom of heaven.' From the Aramaic, there are many translations. His teaching was to all who listened. He blessed all who lived in humility; everyone who knew that their only possession was their breath. Blessing, maturity, ripeness is upon all people who breathe with grace and gratitude. In this same message, he said that the pure in heart are blessed and it is they who will see God. Translations from Aramaic:

'Aligned with the One are those whose lives radiate from a core of love; they shall see God everywhere.'

'Happy and ripe are those who have softened what is rigid within them. They shall be illuminated by a flash of lightning.'

He taught about your soul's journey on the path of humility, meekness, mercy, peace, compassion, and working for justice.

Yeshua showed the *way* of love from his life; he showed the *truth* of how to live in harmony, by his teachings; and he showed that the *life* everyone seeks is a renewed life that comes only after dying to self, day after day. Living as he lived brings one into communion with the Beloved and all creation. In Aramaic the prefix 'b', has many translations, 'through, among, along with, in and like. Anytime he said to believe in him, he said to believe like him. As was the custom in Yeshua's time, and still today in many circles, spiritual seekers who believe in a teacher, try to live like them, pray like them, and even walk like them.

Many of his followers, both men and women, were the people of Israel, present day Jews. He honoured the love they had for Alaha. Those of you, who strive to follow Yeshua, follow him well. Follow him by honouring women, respecting your Jewish brothers and sisters, and by honouring all who love God. To my Christian friends I ask, at what moment did it not become OK to follow the path of Judaism? Yeshua was taught the customs and rituals of the people of Israel. Israel by definition means to wrestle with God. All those who struggle to understand the Beloved are Israel; everyone who wrestles with Truth. As all stories, the story of Israel is your story. It is one story. There is one Beloved. Yeshua said he was one with the Beloved. Unity with Alaha, Sacred Unity, is the reward of all those who wrestle to know the One – all who are Israel.

In the life and work of Yeshua, everything he said and everything he did was to bring you back into unity. He spat on the ground and healed the blind eyes so you would see again your connection to Mother Earth. He healed the deaf and said, "Ethphatah!" 'May the way be opened!' May the sacred path be opened to you as you hear the Sacred Voice. He resurrected Lazarus because Lazarus was his friend. Whenever he had time he would go and visit him. I know how much you lack the intimacy of true friends. As you come back to intimacy with your own soul, your friendships will be restored. He raised a young girl at the prime age of twelve back to life to help you see the grave darkness that is stealing the precious life of so many teenagers. They need their souls resurrected. And the one he rose was a little girl, another sign of the need to awaken to the Divine Feminine.

I am Hokhmah and my table is full of abundant delicacies for you. It has always been here. In Yeshua, I gave many parables about calling everyone to the banquet feast, to the marriage supper. The business and the pre-occupied parts of your inner selves may not see the need to come. That is fine. Bring the wounded, weak, uncertain parts of your souls to my table. Here at the table of abundance is everything you need: strength, joy, healing, courage and here is the cup of remembrance. Sip from it as often as you want until you remember who you are. Oh and it is fun here. There is music, dance, and celebration continually. The wonderful thing about living in Sacred Unity is the bliss. There is so much joy to be Home, knowing Home is in the depth of your soul, and reaches out to the expanse of the Universe. The more you are nourished and the joy of being alive has been restored, you will want to help others to come Home too.

Yeshua left you a prayer and said that if you would pray in his 'shem' (his name, his experience of the One, his essence) that this would help you to unite with the Holy One as He did. The first two words were *Abwoon d'bashemaya*. You have translated this as 'Our Father which art in Heaven'. From the Aramaic it means,

'Oh Breathing Life, your Name shines everywhere.'
'Wordless Action, Silent Potency – where ears and eyes awaken, there heaven comes'

In the ancient languages such as Aramaic, the letter, the sound of the letter, how to make the sound, the numeric value, and the sound of the entire word, was all part of a mystical experience. The first letter is Aleph. The second letter is Bet, and to make this sound, you need to pucker your lips and blow – as if blowing a kiss! Yes, there is the kiss of intimate intention in the first word of the prayer he left you. The Beloved, the Great Mystery, has birthed all that is, and has birthed you, with a kiss. Live in the kiss. Look for the kiss in everything. Make your Home in the wonder of divine affection, the harmony of an entire Universe communing in intimacy.

Yeshua's final prayer was a plea for unity. He asked the Beloved to make everyone one. His life and his teaching were all about the call to unity and harmony. Sometimes he called Beloved, *abba, daddy,* and other times he called the One, *Alaha, Sacred Unity*. That is still the Name of God that Aramaic Christians use today. Allah, Sacred Unity is derived from Alaha, and is the Name of the Beloved that Muslims use. In the Quran, Yeshua has more holy names than any other prophet: *Ruah Allah (Breath of the One); Messiah (al Masih); Servant ('abd Allah); Word (kalmia)*, and many more.

The one word Yeshua used more than any other was *malkutah*. It has been translated as kingdom/queendom. It means 'vision of peace and harmony', the 'I can' of the Cosmos, or the 'reign of unity here and now'. He often referred to the malkutah within and among. The more that peace and harmony reign within you, the more it flows out abundantly from you. He prayed that the realm of heaven here and now would come in urgency. 'Teytey'; come, really come.

The closing of this prayer in English says, 'For Thine is the kingdom, the power and the glory'. In the Aramaic:

'Metul delahe malkutah, wahaylah, wateshbuktah'.
'From You arises every vision and in the vision is the power and the song."

From the depth of your soul, from the Beloved, this tear, this dream of Heaven on Earth arises, and your unique vision of participation in this dream flows forth. In the vision of creating Heaven here and now, is the very power to make it happen. And as it happens for you, you have a new song to sing – with each dream as it comes true. If you can see it, and if you can dream it, you have the power to do it, and the song to flood your soul with bliss.

My friends, so many are looking for the end of all things because they have lost hope. As you stir up the dream within you, you will live it, and the more people who live it, the more contagious living in love and harmony will become. In truth it is what you all desire. It's the Dream. In the book of Thomas, the disciples asked Yeshua about what the end would be like. He said, "Have you discovered, then, the beginning, that you look for the end? For where the beginning is, there will the end be." It is to the beginning that we will turn next: the beginning of it all, and the beginning of your soul's journey.

Reflection: Picture Heaven on Earth now. What does it look like? How can you make this a reality?

Say the word, 'Abwoon' a number of times. (Ahhh —bw(pucker lips as if blowing a kiss) oooo – n. Oh Breathing Life, Radiant One, Birther of the Cosmos.

❦ ❦ ❦

Raptured in the Kiss

I am the life in your Life;
Together we breathe.

I am the giving in your Giving:
Together we receive.

I am love in your Love;
Together we know.

I am peace in your Peace;
Serenity flows.

Oh my Beloved
What joy is this?
Ever living,
Ever loving,
Raptured in the kiss.

I am what You are,
For that is all there is.
Ever living,
Always loving,
Raptured in the kiss.

(May, 2010)

The Soul's Journey

This wonderful Universe story is nothing less than the miraculous story of everything. All of creation is a living adornment of a Dream that seemed too impossible. But, here it is! Here is the living Earth, water, forests, mountains, and all manner of species. Every organism celebrates its own uniqueness and lives in connection with the Whole. The Dream is true! You, beloved ones, are part of this great Dream. Let me tell you this wonderful story again, as your soul's journey. There are a million stories to describe your journey, but again, I will use a story you are familiar with, the Genesis story. Genesis speaks of seven *'yeoms'* translated as 'days'. This word can also be translated as 'periods of illumination'. I present them as seven principles of creation that give wisdom for your soul's journey Home.

Before the journey: Tear – Time for dreams and imagination.
Principle One: Darkness to Light; Pain to Healing; Fear to Truth; Chaos to Clarity
Principle Two: Invisible Realm – Faith; Expectation; Dream.
Principle Three: Realm of Tangible Creation – Dream awakening with Patience.
Principle Four: Cosmic Illuminations – Four Directions (Sun, Moon, Stars, Personal Radiance)
Principle Five: Creativity in the Waters of the Divine Feminine
Principle Six: Creativity in the Earth of the Sacred Masculine
Principle Seven: Home – Wholeness – Peace

In the Tear

I am the door to the realm of sacred Mystery. I am the Way of Peace and Compassion. Before the Before I am. What a joy to enter time and space with you, and the entire Universe. It is such a tangible celebration of Beauty. Every Creation is a unique gift to us. You are so very special, keepers of the Sacred Tear. It is Beloved's Breath that you breathe, my Sap that flows through your veins, and Binah's Water that you hold. Our Wisdom, Compassion, and Intelligent Beauty are tucked away in every cell, and in all of your invisible souls. We do not know how your life will unfold. You are our seed planted in Earth. We watch from within and without in great anticipation.

Children are a delicate treasure to us. They are a reward to the Beloved for having such a marvelous Dream. Every infant, boy, and girl needs to spend their early days in the *tear*, dreaming, imagining, and creating. There is nothing more sacred and important to children than to know the sacredness of their dreams, the innocence of their imaginations, and the joy of their creativity. Childhood years are as sacred as the sacred tear itself. This is the time to connect with the treasure of their longings. They are not ready to embark on their soul's journey. No. They need to be introduced to the vastness of this Universe, to explore, and discover Its Beauty. Every child should feel safe and loved, and be taught the tools of

Wisdom. Many preparations are needed for this adventure on the River of Life.

As the entire Universe lives in community, the Beloved did not foresee that humans would come to the place where they would lose community and live in such isolation. No one suffers because of this more than children. An African proverb says that it takes an entire village to raise one child. This is absolutely the truth. Not one parent can pass on all the tools necessary for a child's journey. In a village, one elder knows all the medicines, another tells the funniest stories, and another has such wisdom, and on and on. With this loss of community, a child's sense of identity is limited to his or her experiences within their particular family unit. Any lack of love and attention, any ill treatment acts like toxins poisoning their sense of self worth and self love, too often for their entire lives. They choose employers and friends who repeat the pattern of their pain. When they look for a lover to share life with, they most often attract another who also lacks self-love.

Let me explain it to you like this. There is a beautiful organization called Hope International that has a passion to help the global population to have access to clean water. Many years ago, they built a well in a small village in Ethiopia. When the local village man saw the water, he wouldn't touch it. The water he had been drinking and using for all of his life was brown! The development worker had to drink it and show him that it was good. The people in the village couldn't recognize this strange, clear substance and had no reference point to cause them to trust it.

This is the reality for so many. Many precious souls have grown up in circumstances that have been less than loving. Love is brown for them, and they attract someone who drinks brown water too. No matter how cruel their circumstances were as a child, it is familiar, and they are drawn to that familiarity in another. It is how the Universe works; like attracts like. In the Universe, this attraction is a celebration of creativity at work. For the many dear people who are more acquainted with fear and pain than love, this attraction acts like a curse to them: loneliness attracts loneliness; fear attracts fear; neglect brings neglect, and so on. Heartbroken souls call out to the Beloved in bewilderment and dismay – how could this happen again? There is nothing Beloved can do. It's about finding the courage to face the brown water and discern it from the pure.

Community for the Natives was not just the entire human community but all of life. The elders would gather the entire village together in the morning to thank the Creator for the day, and to thank the Rain, the Thunder, and Mother Earth. Celebrations and rituals marked a child's journey. The support and love from the community anchored a child in his or her own sense of belonging. That community included all of Nature. Mother Earth was Home to all, and all creatures were regarded as sacred.

With such a loss of community, children grow up wounded, feeling terribly alone, and confused. I wish it weren't so. Remember, I bore humanity in my Essence. When you ache, I ache. There is nothing and no one I ache more for than my little beloveds. They are so impressionable, so innocent, and trusting. The tear has found a new home, and is delighted with new possibilities of creativity and wonder. Children, so full of imagination are capable of dreaming up anything. I wish every precious child was raised in love and harmony. With no concerns for love, safety or protection, they could spend their days in divine captivation of the splendour of this Universe, and dream endlessly about what life has to offer them.

My cherished ones, the Dream doesn't change. It has the same power as it always has. You have lost community – you can build community again. You need each other. Make opportunities for community wherever you can: your places of worship, schools, centres, neighbourhoods, and so on. Engage in discussions that concern you. Build trust among yourselves, so that you can share your inner journeys. Meditate together and share your dreams. As you build community for yourselves, you are building it for the children.

Your education system is a peculiar thing. There is so much emphasis on what you can do behind a desk! Make each classroom an event of discovery. Find ways to facilitate more and more experiences of forests, water, animals, and even the night sky. Let the older mentor the younger on their paths. Create an education system that produces children who are wise in all areas of life.

Help the children to be grounded in love and respect for the Beloved, and all sacred Creation. Amuse them with thousands of creation stories, stories of the Beloved, heroic quests, myths, and fantasies. They receive my wisdom so readily, and their hearts are easily captivated in awe of the Beloved. Consider the Beloved as water and you are a fish, what kind of fish would you be and where would you swim? Look at the Beloved as a Garden, which flower would you be? How would you tend the Garden? What weeds are trying to choke your sense of well-being? Is the ground soft enough for your roots to grow down deep into the heart of the Beloved within you? Can you appreciate the flowers all around you, the ones that are very different from you?

The Divine Clown

You could say Beloved is a Clown. The one thing a clown is interested in is laughter; everything about the Clown is to make all creation happy and happy together. Any clown has many balloons. Master Clown has billions of balloons. It breathed into Earth and Earth is. Divine Clown has breathed into millions of species over billions of years. She breathed into one balloon, shaped it into a tree, another into a dolphin, another into a grasshopper, and so on. All species breathe her Breath. Is the dolphin the Clown? Yes and no. It is distinctly a dolphin, but Clown's breath gives it life. And so all living creation breathes in It and with It. Yet, Clown is greater than all of creation put together. It breathed into you and made you an understudy clown. Maybe this Clown is more of a He, than a She or an It, because He loves to tease, and it seems that all boys love to tease. (And most of them never grow out of this love, so daughters beware!) Clown loves to play 'hide and go seek'. It lets you study It. Then It hides. You look and you look, and then one day you find It hiding behind a big rock. Another time you find Clown hiding in a cave? You were so afraid to go into the cave, but you did, and now that fear is gone!

There are many other clowns who promise to make you happy, but they are all false. One says that if you have the right body image, you'll be happy. Another says that if you have lots of money, you will be happy. Other clowns have long washed off their clown faces, and are sad and even mean. They tell you that there is no happiness in this life. Just give up, or take this happiness in a pill. But don't listen to any of them. Love the Divine Clown and follow only the Clown's voice.

On and on you go on your journey, refusing to listen to the false clowns. You discover more and more of Clown's hiding places. One moment, when you least expect it, Clown takes you by the hand. It tells you that there are no more hiding places; you know them all. You have conquered so many fears, overcome so much pain and you chose love all along the way. You try to remind Clown about all those times you messed up. Clown doesn't remember. It only sees your sincere heart in this moment. Clown takes you to a River, and says that it is time to wash off the clown make up; you have your own true smile now. So you both bathe, and you see! You see your reflection and Clown's reflection are the very same! What a marvel! What joy! You continue on your journey with such a feeling of bliss. You and the Clown are one. You give love and laughter to everyone and everything you meet in your own unique way. No one laughs quite like you!

You have many creative stories to tell children to help them embrace the Beloved. Remember, the first call of the tear is to know Her again. Every time you tell stories of the Beloved, that call is answered. What would the world be like if the children loved the One Beloved, and were raised knowing that they are miracle reflections of this Divine Being?

And then there is Me, Wisdom. The more children have the opportunities to experience their awe of the Universe, and love of the Beloved, the more my Presence is welcomed. I come with Her. How would you describe Me? Beloved is the Fire, I am the Flames, and Beauty is the Heat. Beloved is the Wind, I am the Breath lost in the Wind and Intelligent Beauty is the invisible Evaporation that rises in adoration to Her, and then falls in Condensation, caressing the Earth. Beloved is the Ocean. I am the Current, and Beauty is the Waves. Every child has one droplet reserved just for them. But that droplet is enough to swim in, splash, draw up a well, and fill a river to carry them through a very adventurous life. Invite the children to engage in Mystery. There is nothing more worthy of your time. Einstein said, 'Imagination is more important than knowledge'. Telling stories to the precious little ones will also keep you young at heart and flame your love of the Beloved!

What has been lost can be regained. As it has come forth from the Universe, it is still in the Universe, ready to be accessed. Community has been lost and can be restored. Take every opportunity to build Heaven on Earth with the dear little ones in as many creative ways as you can imagine. Humanity can be a family again. I am with you. I have always been with you. You can learn of Me and you will find me gentle and lowly of heart. I love you all so very much. Come Home together. Bring all of the children. Let's play.

Reflection: Take every opportunity to spend time with the children in your life. Engage in their imaginations. Help them build their connection to Earth, Elements, and species.

Dig up old creation stories from many traditions and tell these and your own stories about the Creator and Creation.

Those of you who have a passion for the education system, transform it to be meaningful in every aspect. Your tear will guide you.

I pray

God

To

Rid me of

God.

Meister Eckhart
(Fox 1983, p. 50)

The seed of God is in us,
Now

the seed of a pear tree
grows into a pear tree;
and a hazel seed
grows into a hazel tree;

a seed of God
grows into
God.

Meister Eckhart
(Fox 1983, 28)

Imagination

is not a talent of some,

But is the

health

of everyone.

Ralph Waldo Emerson

Chaos to Clarity

When Beloved kissed the tear, the Universe was born. I flared forth like the heated flames of a dragon's breath. It was dark and chaotic. The comfort of the Dream was quickly forgotten. There was no *time* to figure out what was happening; we were racing far passed the clock. We gathered unto ourselves galactic clouds, the womb of the galaxies. It was almost ten billion years before the fiery light of the sun. It takes a lot of faith and a tremendous amount of patience to make it through the darkness!

The Womb of Life is a dark and chaotic place. Whether it is the explosion of a supernova, the death of a star, or the bursting of the Tear, it is a tough experience. And so it is for you. One's identity is shattered. Comforts are lost. Everything that was once familiar seems distant. It is the worst alone feeling anyone can have. Your heart is broken. You feel uncertain. The former happiness and security has quickly vanished. You're caught in the middle of what was and what is not yet. Nothing seems to make sense and life is crazy. How could this be a good experience? But it is. For you, it's called death, the dark night of the soul. Whether it is a seed in the ground, or a caterpillar wrapped in a cocoon, a strange metamorphosis takes place, and it seems there is nothing to hold onto. Every soul passes this way many times. It's the alchemical process that refines and brings transformation – pain.

When anything in the Universe dies, it just dies. There is an immediate surrender to the womb of darkness; death is never an end, just a passage to a new beginning. You, on the other hand, can resist inner death; it often seems too difficult to surrender to pain. Far too many dear souls do everything but the right thing when they are in pain. They hide it, latch onto someone to be a new source of happiness, medicate it for too long, fuel it with anger and blame, or let it depress them, depriving them of hope. The wise response to pain is to be with it. Embrace it. Look for Me, Wisdom. I am there. I am at the heart of all pain. You see my beloveds, pain *always* comes up to be healed; revealing old patterns that are now ready for transformation. My wisdom is the spotlight. You are cosmic beings of radiant light, and nothing is impossible for you. But you are also the keepers of the sacred tear, and that identity as light beings is hidden deep within. Pain takes you to these deep places, and you ask yourself hard questions. Childhood wounds are unearthed as you dig for answers. Beloved Rilke said, "Pain is the best friend of your destiny. Difficulty is the best friend of your soul." Matthew Fox describes creation spirituality as the four paths: *via positiva, via negativa, via creativa,* that leads to *via transformitiva.* Creation is good, positive. Pain, the negative experience, births creativity that transforms you and life around you. Yet, no matter what vernacular, or wise saying, nothing seems to really prepare a soul for my fiery furnace that refines and transforms.

You are not ready for this dark night of the soul until adulthood. With heavy heart, I witness child after child thrown into the chaos at birth. I formed you in my Essence. My living sap flows through your veins. Oh, how I grieve for my little ones. Reach out to as many children as you can. There is such a shortage of love and guidance. Many feel no sense of purpose and their youthful vigor is drained as they get sucked into a black hole; an abyss of endless darkness.

Access as much help as you can as you walk through your pain. There are many more holistic healing methods available now.

Above all, share your pain. Pain needs a voice. It makes the load lighter. Even just a compassionate ear alleviates much of the burden. Be gentle with yourself. Sit in the quiet, and listen. My Wisdom is soothing. Remember, it always gets the darkest just before the dawn. Hold onto your dream. You are experiencing its birth pains.

What you do with your pain, determines *everything*. Many, far too many, dear souls swirl around in the galactic clouds for their entire lives. *Only*, if you embrace the pain and search for the light will you find it. I am so sorry that you have to pass through these dark times, and they last too long. But if you cower, blame, give up hope, ignore or hide the pain, you can spin in chaos all your life, wrapping yourself in one cocoon after another, never experiencing your true beauty. Look at the beauty all around. Consider the gift of each season: the bright colours on the leaves as they die in the fall, the sacred rest of winter, and the renewal and refreshment of spring. The darkness and chaos of pain is a season; something new and wonderful is rising.

Facing your pain is the hardest and longest part of your journey. Remember, we were ten billion years before birthing the Sun, who birthed Earth. As the Sun came before the Earth, so light precedes creativity. This not a linear story, even though it may sound like it is. I can't find a way to help you comprehend no time and no space. I live in that realm as I engage with you. But the reality is that the tear is falling *now*. The Earth is being born in this very moment. The darkness of the galactic clouds and the bursting of the sun's energy kiss each other in every moment; they are a beautiful couple. So, my friends, you don't pass through ages of pain only and then come to a grand enlightenment. You pass this way many times, and usually, each time with more grace. You have learned to be still in your pain. With each alchemical process, the soul returns more and more to its enlightenment. That is my reward. I get lost in the flames of my love for you every time you discover one of my holy sparks. Enlightenment is very personal. No one can give it to you, and you never know when or how it will come. Absolutely, it seems to never come early enough. You think you can't pass through one more day, but you do. You know it is the only right thing to do. It's a tremendous loss when any soul just gives up – please, don't give up. The deeper the pain, the higher you will rise up in your new awareness. It is a promise. The dream of a happy, fulfilling life is yours; it's Mine; it's Binah's; it's Beloved's and every angel around you is loving and helping you on your journey. I promise you that your eye has not yet seen what beauty awaits you. You will be astounded.

Religions err when they do not encourage you to seek. Many religious leaders condense this adventurous journey to a set of rules, creeds, and prayers. If you believe this, do this, pray this way, then you will have God, and you are whole. That is a very strange notion indeed. Go out and catch a Sun's ray and give that to someone. That exercise is just as futile as trying to impart the revelation of the Beloved to someone. Communion with the Beloved is a personal love affair. The delight of her Presence comes to those who pursue Her. I am the One who awakens you to Radiance.

Fears are usually rooted in pain, and it is most often childhood pain. If you didn't experience the love and support from the ones who birthed you, it is very hard to really believe anyone really cares. That is where fears take hold – afraid that no one really loves you; fear of being left alone; fear that you're just not that important, or not smart enough; fear that you will be hurt by the very one you love, and on and on. Fears are impartial. You can be successful, attractive, popular, rich, or sincerely devoted as a lover of Life, and yet inside, feel broken, cold, and terribly alone. There is nothing gentle about fears. They are mean, mocking, and attacking. The deeper the fear, the more torment it has. It is the biggest thief to your sense of well-being, and self-love. Unfortunately, fears are relentless. They won't loosen their grip, or just go away.

As with pain, the best thing to do is face them head on. Always be curious about your pain and fears. 'Why do I feel like this? When did I feel like this before? What do I think will happen?' Children internalize their fears, making it part of their identity. Only pain breaks that false identity open, so you can see it. When you see it, you can let it go. That's not you! You are beautiful and wonderful. Parents can only give you what they have. If they haven't found their own self-love, there is a shortage of the experience of love that they can provide for you. Let them go too. Don't blame them, no matter what they did. There is *no* shortage of Beloved's love for you; *no* shortage of my Wisdom to guide you to the light; *no* shortage of Intelligent Beauty's ability to comfort and reveal your true inner beauty. You deserve to be free! Fears are not you; you are love. Fear has no power over you; you have power over fear. All fears are lies; the opposite is the truth. Remember the River. Keep looking in the River. Your true reflection shows your true beauty, your worth, and your loveliness.

So my beloveds, wherever you are on your journey, be kind to yourself. Everything is OK. You are loved. The search for the Light is ongoing; love the journey. By embracing the quest, you are loving the Beloved, and returning to Her the best gift in the Universe – longing desire. Live with the intention to seek the Clarity of Light in your soul in every moment. This is the first principle of creation: accepting the womb of darkness and the search for the light of Truth. Be mindful always that everything contains the opposite: chaos – clarity; search – discovery; darkness – light; pain – healing; fear – freedom; disease – wholeness; grief - joy. If you have one, you have the other. Wait for it; it will come. You will pass through periods of pain many times, and with each will come the reward of greater enlightenment. It is your desire for the Light that directs your path, and the joy of finding this great Mystery that keeps you determined. It is the making of every quest!

Reflection: Search your soul gently. Examine any area of discontent, pain or fear. Embrace it lovingly. Ask the Beloved to give you clarity and wisdom. Follow your heart. There will be someone to talk to, a book to read, or some other help for your journey.

The Guest House

This being human is a guest house.
Every morning a new arrival.

A joy, a depression, a meanness,
some momentary awareness comes
as an unexpected visitor

Welcome and entertain them all!
Even if they're a crowd of sorrows
who violently sweep your house
empty of its furniture,

still, treat each guest honorably.
He may be clearing you out
for some new delight!

The dark thought, the shame, the malice.
meet them at the door laughing,
and invite them in.

Be grateful for whoever comes
because each has been sent
as a guide from beyond.

Rumi
(Barks 1995,109)

Heal your childhood wounds

Or

Your past

becomes

Your future.

George Bernard Shaw

This above all,
to thine own self
be true.
And it must follow,
as the night, the day,
Thou canst not then
be found
false
with any man.

*Shakespeare (**Hamlet**)*

Surrender

Willingly I fall
deep into the black soil
of emptiness.
It's so dark – so cold.

Slowly
You begin to crack the surface
and peel back layer upon layer
of pain.

Then the worst.
Fear – everywhere.
Laid open – bare – no warmth
No Light.

Forsaken – again!
Alone – again!

I want to run away
from myself.

I scream in torture.

What more can I give you?

I am nothing. I have nothing

Ah yes. I wanted.
But that is Yours too.
I want nothing. OK. I want no one.

Nowhere to run
Just sit, seemingly dead.
But that can't be.
Wouldn't the pain be gone?

Then a little light
and more
I see new potential,
clearer perspective.
Darkness fades.
Suddenly, I see.
I am the light.
It seems now – the world is mine.

Why does it take so long to die,
And a moment only, to be reborn?

May. 2008

Invisible to Visible
Heaven in Earth

The second principle is the realm of heaven. In Hebrew the word heaven, is *shemayim*. In Aramaic, it is *semaya*. In these languages, heaven refers to the invisible realm all around, certainly not a place in the sky. The third principle is the realm of the visible. These principles work together. Consider Earth as a visible Heaven. Let's go back in our story to the Beginning. Everything was in the tear. Then the magic of the kiss happened and Heaven began clothing herself. Heaven became Earth so that Earth could experience Heaven. This story, your story is the continuous working of these two principles.

I am the Living Logos, Eternal Word, Ancient Wisdom. My wisdom is hidden, discovered only by the diligent seeker. But I am speaking plainly to you because of the crisis humanity has caused. Earth has been regarded as a material resource, land to fight over, or a cursed domain of sinners. Heaven, for many, is seen as a paradise where the peace and love that is lacking here will be found, or a place of reward for good behaviour, or right believing. Nothing could be *further* from the Truth. These views of Heaven and Earth have led to the present demise of what this earthly experience was meant to be.

How can you love a poet and not his or her poetry? How can you love a poet and disregard or even destroy his or her poetry? Beloved is the Poet and Earth is her Poetry.

This is the Dream manifest. Beloveds, when someone dies, what do you miss? You know they still exist in the invisible realm. You miss their earthiness: the smell of their hair, the touch of their lips, the warmth of their hugs, and the sound of their laughter. You come from Heaven and return to Heaven. It is only here and now that there are the miracles of touch, taste, sound, smell, and sight.

Let's assume that there is a beautiful picture of a lush forest on the wall. It represents a living reality but in a dimension you cannot reach. All you can do is witness the beauty of this picture; you can't experience it. Then that picture comes to life! It envelops and embraces you. You are in this miraculous forest. You can see and hear the rare birds. You can smell the scent of the pine. A butterfly lands on your shoulder. After some time, you die and go back into the painting on the wall. The picture on the wall is like Heaven, and the experience is Earth. The opportunity to experience this realm of beauty and harmony is now – in this moment, in that Earth suit you are wearing.

Love the poetry! If you are attentive, you will read more poems everyday. The more you do this, the more you realize that you too are a poet. Whatever is in your imagination, you create, and now others can experience the work of your inspiration.

These two principles inhabit this entire story. The Dream came to Life! Wow! Only this planet in the entire Milky Way galaxy has this life. The other planets are rocky or gaseous substances. What a miracle! It is necessary to appreciate the beauty of this Earth experience for the gift that it is, so that you too will see yourself as a gift. I want you to make the very most of this amazing opportunity called life; from the invisible realm to a tangible embodiment; Heaven wrapped in Earth.

These two principles will empower you to fulfill every dream in your heart, and to heal and protect all of living creation to live their dreams.

One hundred billion galaxies and more have all come from One Dream. Whatever is in the sacred tear is a clear message from beyond of what you are meant to do. As in all births, there is an incubation time. With your dreams, no one knows how long that may be. It differs for each person and for every dream. The dream lives in Heaven, in the invisible realm of spirit. As it rises up within you, it moves into your present consciousness. It gets your attention, and you embrace this longing. You prepare yourself with all available resources to fulfill this dream, but it doesn't come automatically. It must move out of the realm of emotion and the rational, back into spirit. It is spirit that gives birth. This too is a difficult process for you, and can be so frustrating. You *know* that you want and deserve this dream. It is real to you. You have done everything possible to prepare for it; you believe in the realm of faith as much as you can. It seems that the wait is just too long. Those mocking voices from childhood pain easily want to hit replay. 'Everyone gets their dream, but you.' It is a battle in the mind and heart. But you mustn't give up. What would you give up to – stagnation; defeat; purposelessness? No. Just keep putting one foot in front of the other. Love your dream! It is yours to create!

Slowly and silently, as emotions and thoughts come to rest, a different kind of awareness comes to be. It is the awareness of Spirit, where everything that was, is, and always will be - *is*. Anxieties, frustrations, and impatience fall away like dead leaves from a tree. You needed those leaves at one time. They were a part of you. That is where you were on your journey at that time. It is all good. But you have grown wiser and stronger now. It is time for those leaves to fall. Winter comes, and there is serenity and a new peace about your dream. Abraham thought he had to make the dream of a son happen, but if he had waited, he would have seen his dream birthed as promised. Moses had a dream of ending oppression. He tried to make his dream happen by his strength, but the dream happened in a far greater way than he could conceive! All of your love and faith can't make your dream happen on your terms, or on your timetable. But as you surrender and grow, your dream *will* happen, and you will be amazed! It will be more than you thought possible! If ever you doubt this, just take a walk in Nature. The Dream of all dreams happened, and your dream is in the big Dream.

Reflection: Preferably in a group, reflect on the different notions of Heaven, and Earth.

Share your dream with trusted friends. Meet regularly to support your dreams.

St Patrick's Deer Cry

I arise today
through strength in the sky:
light of sun
moon's reflection
dazzle of fire
speed of lightning
wild wind
deep sea
firm earth
hard rock.

St. Patrick – 5th Century Ireland

The Search for You

You are the Cosmic Thread
weaving all creation
into a tapestry of delight.

You are the stars
that shine,
and the darkness of night,

The waves of the ocean
and a drop of water
as it kisses the land.

You are the shore,
a comfort to walk,
and a pebble of sand.

You! You!
Oh how I searched for You!
My soul longed to know You.
I was consumed;
I was desperate.
I looked for You
As if You were somewhere,
in some place,
at some time,
a moment of true encounter.

All I found was confusion,
and unrest.
I loved You at my worst.
I loved You at my best.
Nothing!

Then,
Like a summer breeze,
a flash of lightning,
a Lover's tease,
a Dream awakening,
there You were,
everywhere,
every place,
every time.
You!

Feb. 2005

Cosmic Illuminations

SUN, MOON and STARS

*T*he fourth *yeom* refers to the Sun, Moon, and stars. This principle is intended to give you constant encouragement on your journey. The Sun is a reminder of the faithfulness of the Beloved, and the constancy of Life's embrace. He so generously transforms four million tonnes of himself into light every second. You breathe in that warmth, that radiance with every breath. As you cannot separate the light from the air, you cannot separate Compassion from Breath. The Moon, on the other hand, reflects the ever-changing seasons and cycles of life. As you breathe in the darkness, you breathe in unfolding Mystery. The stars direct your attention to the vast Universe of galaxies, planets, and the billions of stars, each with their own message of delight. And you are a light. Every person in every generation is amazed at these lights. No one has ever tired of experiencing the sun rise, a sunset, the moon in its phases, a starry night, or the radiance of an enlightened soul. I, Wisdom, burn in the Sun, Moon, and stars in my fiery Essence. I will give you a simple ritual that you can do anytime. Rituals honour the connections between the unseen and seen realms.

Face the East and welcome the Sun, energy of yellow, the power of eagle, with its keen perception, strength of flight, and watchfulness. Think of the fresh start of every day, and the new opportunities. Welcome new vision and ideas for your journey.

Turning clockwise, face the West. Welcome the Moon, energy of black, the power of black bear, who is at home in caves. Embrace the power of intuition, the mystical, and the dark womb of new beginnings. Reflect on the changes life brings, and welcome the changes you are experiencing now.

Turn one-quarter turn to the North, and welcome the vast expanse of the Universe, the energy of the stars and planets, the power of white, the energy of buffalo. This is the direction of strength.

Clockwise, turn to the South. Welcome the realm of emotions, the playful spirit of coyote, and mouse, and the power of red. Red is for love and red is for blood — a symbol of pain. Love and pain school you in your emotions so that you can shine as a light. Embrace the light that you are.

To complete this ritual, stand in the centre. With arms reached up thank all in the invisible realm that help you on your journey. Then with hands on the Earth, thank Mother Earth. To close, reverently put your hands on your heart connecting with your inner realm. Breathe deeply and with gratitude.

Immerse yourself in this Universe story. Sit at the feet of cosmologists and further your amazement at the vastness of the galaxies. Humans are easily led into deception when they remove themselves from the wonder of this Great Expanse. It is a strange temptation to choose to live in a small controlled world of business and manufactured pleasure, rather than flowing in synchronicity with an entire galaxy! Gazing at the sunrises, sunsets, stars, and the phases of the moon expand your consciousness. More and more you become aware of a Life force that fills you with awe. When you are in awe you capture Me, Wisdom, by osmosis, and Radiance permeates your being effortlessly. It is the greatest surrender you can ever know — yielding your life experience as a willing child of the Universe.

Reflection: As often as you can, be attuned to the sun at dawn and dusk, and the phases of the moon. Learn as much as you can about astrology, astronomy, and cosmology. View pictures of the galaxies. Gain access to a telescope. Teach the children about the Universe at large and be amazed together.

Creativity from the Waters of the Divine Feminine And the Land of the Sacred Masculine

On the fifth day, the Beloved said for the waters to bring forth life. I am Hokhmah, and some call me Sophia. In Essence, everything is a union of all that is feminine, masculine and neither. When it comes to creativity, it comes forth first from the feminine. There was life in the waters for billions of years before on the land. Your life comes forth from the protective amniotic sack in a mother's womb. Long, long ago, ancient people, those on the Isle of Crete, for example, honoured the Divine more in feminine terms, because of the fertility of Earth. Cultures enjoyed a greater measure of peace, and creativity flourished. This fifth principle reveals the connection between the feminine and creativity.

Be it the artist's brush, sculptor's hand, writer's pen, movement of dance, or other, all creativity is alive with emotion, inspiration, and passion. The desire to express is like the current pulsating from the heart, through deep emotions, to mind, to body. Inspiration and creativity flow like a gentle brook or a cascading waterfall. This yearning to express has a life of its own and can't be contained. With every burst of creativity, is a new joy; a unique expression from the great unknown.

Think of the tear, that pool of primordial water! It is the tear within you that calls you to bring forth. It is that River of Life that draws you to a clearer and clearer reflection of yourself, in your true beauty. Beauty loves to be expressed!

The very element of water is refreshing, and cleansing, bringing new vitality. Creative expression is like that. Without water, there is no life; without inspiration, there is no creativity. Everyone should create all the time. There is nothing more for me to say here; creativity can't be taught nor dictated. Enjoy! No one feels more alive than when they create. And, I'm always mindful of the children. Bring as much creativity back into the schools as you can.

Then Beloved asked the land to bring forth. This is the sixth principle, which flows from the fifth. Land without water is parched and nothing can grow. Masculine energy without the feminine lacks the creative juice; but in balance with the feminine, offers millions more opportunities for new expressions. The Sacred Masculine is connected to and even entwined with Mother Earth as depicted in the ancient symbol of the Green Man who loved the Earth and protected all that was nourished by Her. Earth is firm, and dependable to support all who walk upon It, very different from the element of water. Masculine creativity displays itself in concrete formulas, measurable sciences, and rational rhetoric.

To replace the unjust systems of this world with new systems established on principles of compassion, justice, and equality for all, will take the integrity of the Sacred Masculine. The Sacred Masculine that is in balance with the Divine Feminine is ingenious, strong, fearless, protective, and full of fervent compassion. You could liken the Divine Feminine to the melody and the Sacred Masculine provides the notes on the page. You can harmonize easily with the melody, unless you have lost your voice, or are too afraid to sing. The Sacred Masculine in its firm and concrete effectiveness teaches you how to sing again.

Modern culture is based on consumerism; to consume means to 'eat up' or destroy. Mother Earth is being destroyed by life styles that take from Her endlessly, poison her and then shove their waste all over Her in the worst defilement. Beloved human, you are the only species that feeds its predators! Every dollar spent empowers someone. Instead of fueling economic systems that destroy, you could empower yourselves. The Sacred Masculine will inform new ways of business that are sustainable, and bring power back to Earth-based communities, not multi-billion dollar corporations.

Creativity is as endless as your imagination, and as potent as the Dream itself. Anything is possible. Everything is possible. Beloveds, in this time of so much destruction and violence, it will take the vision and creative thrust of many to turn the course of events. The vision has never changed. It is the Dream: Heaven on and in Earth. The more soul work you do, the more you know who you are, and the tear rises up. The call of the Dream compels you to access the eternal resources within you. You see, Beloved wants Her Dream back; the dolphins want to experience their dream; the chimpanzees deserve to frolic in the forest from night to day. You deserve to live your dream — in peace, harmony and beauty. Lay aside any insecurity, or feeling of insignificance. No one can make a difference the way you can.

As you follow your dream of creativity and change, you will meet others with the same passion, and group together. Like the miracle of transformation from single cell to multi-cellular organisms, you will organize, form co-operatives, and will network to create a living force of transformation in the world. There are far more loving people in the world, than those who have sold their souls for greed and power. My call is to all loving people to listen intently. As more and more good-hearted people wake up to my stirrings, the depth of wisdom that will flow, the strength of courage, and the wealth of creativity *can* restore *malkutah* Heaven on Earth, here and now.

Reflection: What passion calls you? If you could change something about society at large, what would that be? Give time to ponder how you could bring about these changes, and group with others with the same passion.

Explore and enjoy your own creativity.

❦ ❦ ❦

The two – the hero and his ultimate god,
the seeker and the found
are thus understood as the outside and inside
of a single, self-mirrored mystery,
which is identical
with the mystery of the manifest world.
The great deed of the supreme hero
is to come to the knowledge of
this unity in multiplicity
and
then to make it
known.

Joseph Campbell
(Campbell 1949, 40)

Today, like every other day,

we wake up empty and frightened.

Don't open the door to the study

and begin reading.

Take down a musical instrument.

Let the beauty we love be what we do.

There are hundreds of ways

to kneel and kiss the ground.

Rumi
(Barks 1997, 36)

*Creativity From The Waters Of The Divine Feminine
And The Land Of The Sacred Masculine*

Soul of the World

Soul of the world,
no life, no world remains;
no beautiful men and women longing,
Only this ancient love circling the holy, black stone of nothing

Where the Lover is the Love,
the horizon, and everything within.

Not until someone dissolves, can he or she know
what union is,
that descends only into emptiness.
A lie does not change to truth
with just talking about it.

A poet tries to say Love's Mystery,
why the reed flute grieves.
Listen and obey the hushed language.
Go naked.

As salt dissolves in ocean,
I was swallowed up in God,
beyond doubt, or being sure.

Suddenly, here in my chest
a star came out so clear;
It drew all other stars into me.

Love told me to reject mind,
and also spirit.
"Live with me."
For a while I did.
Then I left, and came back,
and left again.
Now I'm here to stay.

Looking for the ocean,
I find a shell with a piece of foam on it.
I taste the ocean in the foam.
I turn within.
A distant trail opens out on a high ground.

Rumi
(Barks CD, 2002 #4)

Home

*B*efore the Before, was the tear – the great longing. From that tear, you came forth and you are the trusted species that holds this tear. The tear has called you, led you out of chaos into the light, brought forth so many dreams into the realm of experience, and has inspired ingenious and artistic expressions. There is an intimate communion that develops with this tear. Its mystery intrigues you. It came from the depth of the Beloved's longing. I waited in Silence, for the kiss. I was the heat that flared forth. All of that loving memory lives in the tear; it holds the memory of the Dream – the Dream of it All.

The reward of honouring the tear is that it brings you home. Home is where you enjoy the seventh principle of creation – peace and rest. Home is the true reality of who you really are. Here, there is great contentment and comfort; here there is the soul's peace, flowing in harmony with all that is, seen and unseen. Living in loving embrace of your soul's journey, brings the awakening of being home in greater measures moment by moment. Meister Eckhart was aware of this principle when he said to you, "God is at home. It is we who have gone out for a walk."

Remember the grand event that happened six hundred thousand years ago. Light sensitive eyespots developed into eyes and Earth saw herself for the first time. The more you travel this soul's journey; the more you become sensitive to the Light. Gradually, or sometimes suddenly, often in a moment unexpected, an amazing transformation occurs and you *see* yourself, as if for the first time! You know that you are one with the Beloved; one with all creation; one with the entire Universe. It is a blissful peace; you are grounded in your own sense of being, and ecstatic that this very essence is the only Essence!

It is I, Hokhmah, who calls you home in the tear. I am the One who gathers all back into unity and harmony. I birthed you in my Essence, and walk with you through all the dark passages. I long for you to experience being Home in greater and greater dimensions of awareness. Home, the hearth of love is always lit. You partake freely from my table of abundance. Home is Truth; Home is Love; Home is Peace. If your journey has been very hard, you can rest now. There is always more to journey through, but it will be softer now. If your beginnings lacked love, you have endured broken relationships. Now you will attract a lover who is also home. As like attracts like, you will attract love to yourself. The Universe lives in an endless dance of attraction. You can spin and twirl around with us. What a delight. Enjoy the dance!

I have poured myself out for you in this story. Every word is a gift of wisdom, love and grace. What is more important is the space between the words. That is more of a gift; that is the Beloved breathing life into you, breathing love into you. You, my precious friend, are the loved, the loving and love itself – you. I have chosen to speak plainly to you for two main reasons, although the reasons are many.

I want you to come Home, and here experience that the Beloved is good – only good. I want you to know who you are. I want you to enjoy being alive. You deserve all of Love's best. I want you to breathe deeply and freely, and enjoy the love of others, of a lover, and the love of all creation. The first reason is just that – love for you because you are worth it. The second reason is love for the gift of Earth. If you could experience the complete agony of Mother Earth, you could not bear it. Even one small portion of her agonizing pain would break your heart into a million pieces and you would go crazy; your body could not bear the intensity of the grief and groaning of Earth.

Mother Earth needs you; I need you to become active participants in healing Her. I say Her, but it is I. We are One, for One is all there is. Beloved, Intelligent Beauty and I, Wisdom are One. We worked, danced and played together cloaking our Dream into this miraculous dimension. We are the 'I AM'. I am Beauty; I am Beauty in Earth. I am Life. As Earth I live. As water I live. As mountains I live. And I ache deliriously. As Mother Earth, I have been so generous to all but humanity takes, kills, steals and destroys. The spirit that fuels modern civilizations, which are barely civil at all, is not the spirit of love.

Wherever you are on your journey, I implore you to live with intention. Before you buy anything, know where it comes from. Know what the making of that product has done to Mother Earth. Think about what you will do with that product when it becomes waste. Do you really need it? Who will profit from that purchase? When you see paper and wood, think of the trees. And then there is life's precious gift of water. How is She being honoured? Where and how is your food grown? Are you wasting our gifts? By keeping these questions in your consciousness, and acting accordingly, you are loving Mother Earth.

Hearken to my Voice and you will find the wisdom and courage to take action and stop the destruction. The systems of this world are like the airplane I already mentioned. Not only is it out of balance due to patriarchy and abuse of power, it is also headed in the wrong direction. It cares not about the destruction it has already caused and that will bring its end, taking the Beauty of Earth and all of life with it. Far too many humans just shrug their shoulders and continue living in the same uncaring manner, and others look for an end in 2012 or some apocalypse. With this thinking, I grieve all the more. But you, my caring listener, as you focus your soul on

Home (heaven within and without), you are already there. Your loving attention creates the reality.

My wisdom is displayed in the heavens. The vastness of Beloved, Wisdom and Beauty is spread across billions of galaxies. This compassion and wisdom is available to all, and it is enough, more than enough to bring Malkutah – heaven here and now. Will you answer the call? You will have to become still and listen. Life in this present age is far too busy and noisy. You were not made to live in that way. Notice the stillness and quiet of Nature. There is your true mode of being. Come my beloveds, although the ways of humankind are like scarlet, you and I *will* make them white as snow. For this, from my heart of hearts I thank you. Beloved hugs you. Intelligent Beauty kisses you. And Sacred Earth and all species will show their gratitude in their living.

Reflection: How much do you really love yourself? How much do you really love this Earth Home? Spend as much time as you can in silent listening.

Love after Love

The time will come when,
with elation,
you will greet yourself
arriving at your own door,
in your own mirror;
And each will smile at the other's welcome,
and say,
'Sit here. Eat'.

A Story to Live By

You will love again
the stranger who was yourself.
Give wine. Give bread.
Give back your heart
to itself,
to the stranger who has loved you all your life;
whom you ignored for another.
who knows you by heart.

Take down the love letters from the bookshelf,
the photographs,
the desperate notes.
Peel your own image from the mirror.
Sit, feast on your life.

Derek Walcott

Welcome Home

Welcome Home
my dear one,
welcome Home.
How long I have waited for you;
how my heart ached
as I saw you in pain,
hiding in the closet of human suffering.

One by one
I led you to the rooms of your true abode;
this Palace of Wonder,
called a Soul.

So shy and timid,
at first you were,
even fearful;
too hard to believe that any of this
belonged to you.

Cowering in unworthiness,
shaking in fright,
wallowing in loneliness,
you took my hand and held on tight.

You would open your eyes,
just a little, here and there.
A foreign place it seemed.
But you have such faith.
You took the dare.

Now each room
is fully lit.
Comfort at last,
peace and bliss.

Let's sit now,
by the hearth
of Love come Home
You have found your Soul
Sacred and Whole.

May, 2009

May all of your becoming,
Be Coming Home.

Feb. 2009

As it was in the Beginning, is Now

So then, long before the birth of the human; before the flowers arrayed the Earth; before the birds graced the sky; before the appearance of mammals capable of loving; before the crawling species of such delicate features; before the grand forests; and before the swimming life; and long before the birth of this Earth; its Moon; the grandeur of the Sun; the sacrifice of the Supernova; the gathering of the galactic clouds; and Love's fiery kiss; the Beloved was. I, Hokhmah, Wisdom, was there with Her, and Binah, Spirit of Intelligent Beauty was there too. We began to be moved and stirred by a Dream, such a Dream! In one moment, which became the first moment, a *tear* rolled down and Beloved caught this tear. There in this pool of primordial waters She beheld all that She had dreamed, so magnificent, and so entirely precious. She knelt to kiss this tear, but I, the Heat in Her Holy Breath, sent this tear off. And the Universe was birthed with a *kiss!*

Thank-you my dearest and most beloved friends; you have been such attentive listeners. The wonder and beauty of this story, is that it is a living story – a story to live by. It is the story of a Dream awakening unto Itself; it is your story. All I ask you to remember, is that it is *one* story; for all that is has come forth from the One and unto the One all return; in the Life of the One all live; in the Breath of the One, all breathe. And I have one request. Today, tomorrow and every day, greet the morning with hands stretched high, then on your heart, and then touching the Earth, and say this:

Beloved, my Beloved, I say yes!
I say yes to the dream of me!
I say yes!

I say yes to the dream of a loving humanity!
I say yes!

I say yes to the dream of this Earth in all of its lush Beauty!
I say yes!

Teytey Malkutah!
Heaven come to be! Heaven in Earth! Heaven on Earth!
Heaven in me, through me, and all around me!
Desire your Dream through me and
Let the realm of love, harmony and beauty be a reality
for all living creatures, and all of Earth!

I say yes, my Beloved!
I say YES!

A note from the author

I am thrilled and honoured to share this story with you. It is a story that has come in waves and tears over the years. It certainly has taught me so much and is for me, a story to live by. With all of my heart, I do believe we can bring forth Malkutah, heaven here and now. To do that will take all of us with consistent and fervent efforts. One thing is for sure, if we continue living as we have been, we will just get more of the same; we will bring our own destruction. It is so easy to be comfortable and complacent when life is relatively easy. Every moment we wait, precious opportunities are lost.

I see modern culture as a west wind that has been blowing for over two hundred years. It blows in the way of progress, more manufactured goods, more spending, more accumulating, having more technological toys, and even eating more. It has blown a feeling of arrogance, dominance, and violence from the beginning as shown in the deplorable way the natives, the animals and the land were treated. There is a fresh breeze from the east. It is a spirit of simplicity, of kindness to all, of giving as much and as often as one can, of harmony with all of Earth, of restoring and healing what has been lost and broken. Be it human lives without food and water, others who live in fear and with injustice, or living species, waters and Earth, there is a fresh breeze of compassion for all.

Most people would love to flow with this wind from the east. Many already do. We get its attention by living differently in every moment. Many of the changes aren't hard at all. Instead of that extra unneeded snack, or those items of clothing that will mostly sit in the closet etc., you choose to put that money to good use. There

A Story to Live By

are already many great organizations doing transformative work, but they could do a lot more with more funds. Beyond that, is to become active transforming our local communities, and doing all we can on a larger scale. This world does not belong to the greedy and corrupt. They have been running it for far too long. In short, this Earth is Beloved's dream, and She wants Her dream back. We and all species deserve to live our dream. Together we can and will bring forth Malkutah, heaven here and now. I bless you all on your journeys. We are one in this fresh wind that carries us. I wrote this poem in the middle of the night last night. (Oct. 3, 2010)

> *There is a Spirit rising in the East*
> *where the sun does rise*
> *and days are born.*
>
> *Just surrender*
> *and*
>
> *It will sweep you off your feet,*
> *and will direct you*
> *to a greater morn.*

Teytey Malkutah!
Nancy Farishta Nuri

For those who are looking for organizations to support, here are just a few:

David Suzuki Foundation – environmental issues – building an ecologically better future
Council for Canadians – protecting clean water, energy security etc
World Wildlife Fund – protecting wildlife
Amnesty International – human rights
Hope International – wells for the poor
Mennonite Central Committee – a host of projects

A Note From The Author

For retreats on eco-spirituality
Gaia Centre in Halliburton ON
St. Ignatius College in Guelph ON
Genesis Farm in New Jersey

For presentations of this story in various forms, workshops, retreats, or teachings,
Visit my website www.malkutah-heaven.com

References

I chose to put no footnotes for many reasons: they would break the flow of the story, and so many authors and teachings have influenced my work, that it would be hard to distinguish one from another. Also, I thought it would be more beneficial to do a more detailed reference as my bibliography. I can honour these teachers in the context of their own work, and how that has interested and impacted me. This can more adequately direct you toward your specific areas of interest for further investigation.

Kabbalah

The Tree of Life and Ladder of Life presented in the Kabbalah was a teaching restricted to only the most devout male Jews for many centuries. Only in recent years has this teaching been available to all. For a general overview, I would direct you to *The Practical Kabbalah* and for a more in-depth study; Gershom Scholem's work is excellent. He has more books than listed here. Rabbi david cooper's book is wonderful, concise, and with meditations to follow. He also offers retreats, but I have never gone to any of them.

As mentioned in the introduction, at the top of the Tree is Kether, crown, and beneath Kether, forming the base of a triangle is Hokhmah, Wisdom, to the right and Binah, Understanding to the left. This triad is at play throughout my story. I want to be clear that, although I have taken these names from the Tree of Life, this is my creative work and does not reflect the teachings of the Kabbalah. I found congruence between this triad at the top of the Tree of Life with the trinity in the Christian tradition. (Actually there is a triune theme in many religions, and myths.) Rabbi Cooper breaks down the five areas of the human soul as taught in Kabbalah. I make reference to the third area, nashama, in the chapter on the Divine Human. Nashama is the pure essence of every human soul. Chuck Burrack is presently writing a book on creativity and the Kabbalah.

Cooper, David A. *God is a Verb: Kabbalah and the practice of mystical Judaism*, New York: Riverhead Books, 1997.

Epstein Perle. *Kabbalah: The Way of the Jewish Mystic*, Boston & London: Shambhala, 1991.

Hopking, C. J. M. *The Practical Kabbalah guidebook*, New York: Sterling Publishing Co., Inc., 2001.

Scholem, Gershom. *Kabalah: A Definitive History of the Evolution, Ideas, Leading Figures and Extraordinary Infuence of Jewish Mysticism*, New York: Penguin, 1974.

_____,*On the Kabbalah and Its Symbolism*, New York: Schocken Books, 1963.

Aramaic Work

I came across the tape series *'Original Prayer'* in a catalogue from Sounds True in 2001. In this series, Neil Douglas-Klotz teaches the meaning of the words in the Lord's Prayer from the Aramaic language, and also leads in meditations. I have since read all of his books, listened to all the CD's, and have danced the cycle of the Lord's Prayer (and other sacred dances) with him many times. To understand who Jesus, Yeshua, was and what he said, one must put him in his native Middle-Eastern context and listen to him in his language of Aramaic. To attempt to understand him through the lens of Western culture, the English language, and organized religion, would be the same as trying to observe the habits of a dolphin on land. The subject does not fit the context. I owe a lot to Neil's work. The essence of what I have gained from the Aramaic is like an invisible thread that holds this story together. (More than what I can specifically reference). Many of Yeshua's followers thought that he inhabited the Essence of Hokhmah – Holy Wisdom. Yeshua called God *Alaha* (Sacred Unity). That is still what Aramaic Christians call God, and *Allah* (Sacred Unity) is what Muslims call God. The word *malkutah* means *the I can of the cosmos, the vision of unity,* or *heaven here and now* as I have put it. The reference to *dam* in the chapter on the Divine Human, and all of the Aramaic work in the chapter on Yeshua is from Neil's work. His recent research is on the references to Yeshua in the Quran. I cited some of these names from a talk Neil gave in Cairo in 2008. (Possibly Neil will publish a book from this research in the future) There is also a wonderful book on the 99 Names of God in the context of Sufism. The references to the various prayers in the religions in chapter one is from the International Network for the Dances for Universal Peace, which Neil is greatly involved with.

Douglas-Klotz, Neil. *Blessings of the Cosmos; Wisdom of the Heart from the Aramaic Words of Jesus,* Sounds True, Bolder, CO, 2006.

_____ *Desert Wisdom: Sacred Middle Eastern Writings From The Goddess Through The Sufis,* San Francisco: Harper, 1997.

_____ *The Genesis Meditations; A Shared Practice of Peace for Christians, Jews, and Muslims,* Quest Books, Wheaton Illinois, 2003

_____ *The Healing Breath: Body-based Meditations on the Aramaic Beatitudes (CD series),* Sounds True, Bolder, CO, 2004.

_____ *The Hidden Gospel: Decoding the Spiritual Message of the Aramaic Jesus,* Wheaton, Illinois: Quest Books, 1999.

_____, *Original Prayer CD Series,* Sounds True, Bolder, CO, 1990..

_____, *Prayers Of The Cosmos; Meditations On The Aramaic Words Of Jesus,* San Francis, 1990.

_____ *The Sufi Book of Life, 99 Pathways of the Heart for the Modern Dervish,* Penguin Group, New York, 2005.

Foundation Dances & Walks: Dances of Universal Peace (Dance Manual and tapes.). Oklahoma City: Peaceworks, 2001.
Website: www.abwoon.com

Matthew Fox

I was priviledged to do a Doctor of Ministry at the University of Creation Spirituality in Oakland California (presently known as Wisdom University). Matthew Fox was the founding president at that time and it was very meaningful to have so much interaction with this great spiritual thinker and leader. He has devoted his career to unleashing the suppressed mystical and life-affirming traditions within Christianity and other faiths. For those not acquainted with his work, I would recommend 'Original

Blessing'. Many of us in the West have been raised with a fall/redemption theology, including me. Instead of original sin, Mat refers to original blessing. He has more books than listed here. (Mat's books on the mystics will be referenced in that section,) I make the reference to the 'green man' from Mat's latest book on the Sacred Masculine. For those wanting to embrace ecumenism of all spiritual paths, 'One River, Many Wells' is a work of art; the book is divided into themes, with references from each religion on those themes.

Website; www.friendsofcreationspirituality.com (At this website, you can connect with the work of many of the graduates, and with small groups embracing creation spirituality.)

Fox, Matthew. *The Coming of the Cosmic Christ*, Harper, San Francisco, 1988.

_____ *Creativity; Where the Divine and the Human Meet*, Jeremy P Tarcher, Penguin, New York, 2004.

_____ *The Hidden Spirituality of Men; Ten Metaphors to Awaken the Sacred Masculine*, New World Library, Novato Californian, 2008.

_____ *One River, Many Wells*, Jeremy P. Tarcher/Putnam: New York, 2000.

_____ *Original Blessings* Jeremy P. Tarcher/Putnam: New York, 1983.

_____ *The Reinvention of Work; A New Vision of Livelihood for Our Time*, Harper, San Francisco, 1994.

_____ *A New Reformation!* Wisdom, Wisdom University Press, 2005.

_____ *Sins of the Spirit, Blessings of the Flesh; Lessons for Transforming Evil in Soul and Society,* Three Rivers Press, New York, 1999.

_____ *Spirituality Named Compassion; Uniting Mystical Awareness with Social Justice,* Inner Traditions, Rochester Vermont, 1979.

_____ *Wrestling with the Prophets, Essays on Creation Spirituality and Everyday Life,* Jeremy P Tarcher Penguin, New York, 1995.

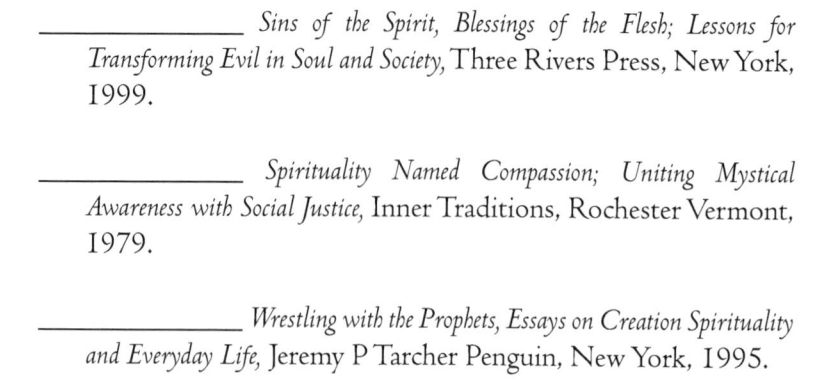

Universe Story

One of the required courses at UCS (University of Creation Spirituality) was New Cosmology. The text was Universe Story, written by Thomas Berry and Brian Swimme. The life-long work of Thomas Berry was to tell the Universe as one story, replacing an all too familiar old story which placed man as the supreme being above all of creation. It has been an honour to hear Brian Swimme in Ohio and Toronto. You can access many teaching DVD's, and books and can sign up for online courses if you visit his website under his name. On page 89, the information about 4 tons of light a second coming from the Sun is from Swimme's book 'The Hidden Heart of the Cosmos', page 39. New Cosmology was my first introduction to the Universe as story. Larry Edwards taught this intensive, which I took twice, and presented this story in tangible and practical ways. He facilitates workshops regularly at Genesis Farm in New Jersey, across the USA, Canada, and Ireland. If you go to his website, you will see many versions of the Cosmic Walk. In my area of Southern Ontario, a cosmic walk was made on the grounds of St. Ignatius College in Guelph in 2009, and dedicated to Thomas Berry, the day before he died. It is a wonderful way of embracing the story of the Universe through ritual, and walking meditation. I am nothing near a scientist, but I have done my best to reflect the work of Berry, Swimme, and Edwards in the telling of the Universe story in chapter 2.

The DVD 'View from the Center of the Universe' is a great teaching tool. The Awakening Universe is a fifteen minute overview of the Universe Story featuring Thomas Berry, Brian Swimme, and others. StarGaze II gives some fascinating photos of our Universe.

Website for Larry Edwards: threeeyesofuniverse.org

Swimme Brian. *The Hidden Heart of the Cosmos; Humanity and the New Story*, Orbis Books, Maryknoll, New York, 2006.

Swimme Brian & Berry Thomas. *The Universe Story; From the Primordial Flaring Forth to the Ecozoic Era; A Celebration of the Unfolding of the Cosmos*, San Francisco, Harper, 1992.

DVD's

Neil Rogin. *The Awakening Universe, A Liberating New Cosmology for Our Time: Based on the 'Universe Story' by Thomas Berry & Brian Swimme*, www.pachamama.org.

StarGaze II; Visions of the Universe. (Access this online.)

Abrams Nancy, and Primack Joel, *The View from the Center of the Universe*, NASA Research Park, Oct.25, 2006.

Mystics

I have been a student of theology, formally and informally all of my life, but was never taught about any mystics. While doing research on the history of pastoral care in 2000, I came across brief references to the Rhineland mystics, and the mystics that influenced Martin Luther. My Lutheran professor allowed me to go outside the norm, and do a paper on the mystics. For the first time, I felt like I had found a home for my spirituality. This began a wonderful and rich journey of discovery. Mystics are those who have dedicated their lives to go beyond belief, into the realm of experience of the Divine. Many of their struggles and sacrifices are recorded. Their love poetry and prose inspires and awakens us to a deeper Love, which is the Essence of Life. As we search for unity and peace in these perilous times, mystics have so much to offer. They are in every spiritual tradition and their heart and voice is in unison – love. I have quotes and poetry from the Sufi mystics: Rumi, Hakim Sanai, and Kabir; and Christian mystics: Hildegard of Bingen, St. John of the Cross, and Meister Eckhart. Because the extensive quote from Hildegard was part of the story, I didn't reference it there. It is from Mat's 'Illuminations of Hildegard' pages 39 & 40, and this work, with its illustrations, is a favourite of many. For a thorough history of Christian mystics, Bernard McGinn's work is phenomenal. The Kabbalah is Jewish mystical teaching, as already stated. Jewish mystic and philosopher Martin Buber has an excellent book 'Tales of the Hasidim'. I will look forward to reading Chuck Barak's forthcoming book on Kabbalah.

An Anthology of Christian Mysticism; The Basic Writings of the Greatest Christian Mystics, Template Publishers

Barks, Coleman, (translations by). *The Essential Rumi,* CastleBooks: New Jersey, 1997.

References

_____ *Rumi; Voice of Longing,* (CD) Sounds True, Boulder CO, 2002.

Besserman Perle. *Teachings of the Jewish Mystics,* SHAMBALA, Boston & London, 1994

Buber Martin. *Tales of the Hasidim,* Schocken Books, New York, 1991.

The Cloud of Unknowing and Other Works, Penguin Books, New York, 1961.

Fox, Matthew. *Hildegard of Bingen's Book of Divine Works with Letters and Songs,* Bear & Company, 1987.

_____ *Illuminations of Hildegard of Bingen,* Bear & Company: Santa Fe, NM, 1985.

_____ *Meditations with Meister Eckhart,* Santa Fe, New Mexico: Bear & Company, 1983.

_____ *Passion for Creation; The Earth-Honoring Spirituality of Meister Eckhart,* Inner Traditions, Rochester, Vermont, 1980.

Griffiths Bede. *Return to the Center,* Templegate, Springfield, Illinois, 1976.

Hemenway, Priya. (translated by) *The Book of Everything; Journey of the Heart's Desire, Hakim Sanai's Walled Garden of Truth,* Andrews McMeel Publishing, Kansas City, 2002.

Julian of Norwich's Showings, Paulist Press, New York, 1978.

Kavanaugh Kieran, & Rodriquez, Otilio. *The Collected Works of St. John of the Cross*, ICS Publications, New York, 1991.

Ladinsky, Daniel. *The Gift: Poems by Hafiz the Great Sufi Master*, U.S.A.: Penguin Comp., 1999.

Larranaga Ignacio. *Brother Francis of Assisi*, MEDIASPAUL, Sherbrooke, QC, The Crossroad Publishing Company, New York, 1998.

McGinn Bernard. *The Essential Writings of Christian Mysticism*, The Modern Library, New York, 2006.

_____ *The Flowering of Mysticism; Men and Women in the New Mysticsm – 1200-1350*, The Crossroad Publishing Company, New York, 1998.

_____ *The Foundations of Mysticism; Origins to the Fifth Century*, The Crossroad Publishing Company, New York, 1999.

_____ *The Growth of Mysticism; Gregory the Great through the 12th Century*, The Crossroad Publishing Company, New York, 1999

Swan Laura. *The Forgotten Desert Mothers; sayings, lives, and stories of early christian women*, Paulist Press, New York, 2001.

Tagore, Rabindranath. *Songs of Kabir: A 15th Century Sufi Literary Classic*, Boston MA: Weiser Books, 2002.

Underhill Evelyn. *The Essentials of Mysticism*, ONEWORLD, Oxford, 1995.

Waddell Helen. (translated by) *The Desert Fathers*, Vintage Books, New York, 1998.

Celtic Spirituality

I came across Celtic spirituality around the same time as the mystics, and soon found these two paths had a lot in common. Celtic spirituality has always embraced love of Nature and love of the human soul in its original goodness. The notion that the soul is completely corrupt is foreign to Celtic thought, (and early Christianity.) Celtic spirituality, like the Celtic knot, weaves the invisible and visible realms together, and it has certainly woven its way into my heart, and this story. Visiting Glendalough, Ireland, the ruins of a monastic community from the 7th century, and St Columba's cave in Scotland were very inspiring experiences. Robert O'Hearn is involved in a thriving Celtic community in Nova Scotia, Canada.

Bradley, Ian. *Celtic Christian Communities: Live the Tradition*, Great Britain: Northstone Publishing. 2000.

Celtic Christianity: Making Myths and Chasing Dreams, Edinburgh: Edinburgh Press, 1999

The Celtic Way, London: Darton, Longman & Todd, 1993.

Cahill, Thomas. *How the Irish Saved Civilization: The Untold Story of Ireland's Heroic Role from the Fall of Rome to the Rise of the Medieval Europe*, New York: Doubleday, 1995.

The Classics of Western Spirituality, *Celtic Spirituality*, New York: Paulist Press. Losack, Marcus and Rodgers Michael, 1999.

Glendalough: A Celtic Pilgrimage, Ireland: Columba Press, 1996

Newell, J. Philip. *The Book of Creation: An Introduction to Celtic Spirituality,* New York: Paulist Press. 1999.

_____ *Listening for the Heartbeat of God,* New York: Paulist Press, 1997

O'Donohue, John. *Anam Cara: A book of Celtic Wisdom,* New York: HarperCollins, 1997.

O'Donoghue, Noel Dermot. *The Angels Keep Their Ancient Places: Reflections on Celtic Spirituality,* Edinburgh and New York: T&T Clark, 2001

Simpson, Ray. *A Holy Island Prayer Book,* Harrisburg, Pennsylvania: Morehouse, Publishing, 2002

Skinner, John (translated by). *The Confession of Saint Patrick,* New York: Doubleday, 1998.

Thames & Hudson. *The Book of Kells,* London: Thames & Hudson Ltd, 1994

Waal, Esther de. *The Celtic Vision: Prayers, Blessings, Songs and Invocations from the Gaelic Tradition,* Missouri: Liguori/Triumph, 1998

References

Karen Armstrong

I highly recommend Karen Armstrong's book on the Battle for God to anyone who has been influenced by fundamentalism in Islam, Christianity, or Judaism. Her research shows the development of fundamental views from the fifteenth century on. This work helped me to understand how the intolerance in fundamental views developed and I agree with her description 'militant piety', as referenced in the chapter on Moses. All of her works are excellent. I am presently reading her book on Muhammad, and as usual is a wonderful and enriching read.

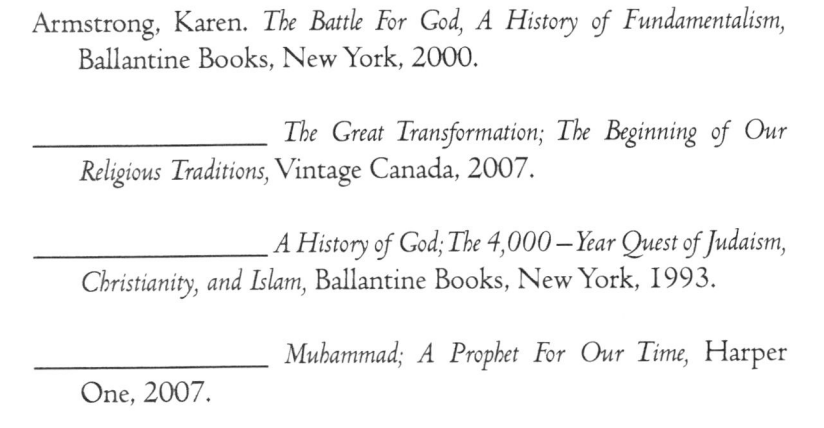

Armstrong, Karen. *The Battle For God, A History of Fundamentalism,* Ballantine Books, New York, 2000.

_____ *The Great Transformation; The Beginning of Our Religious Traditions,* Vintage Canada, 2007.

_____ *A History of God; The 4,000 – Year Quest of Judaism, Christianity, and Islam,* Ballantine Books, New York, 1993.

_____ *Muhammad; A Prophet For Our Time,* Harper One, 2007.

Elaine Pagels

Elaine Pagels is a brilliant scholar. Her research into the early Christian period helped me to clarify where the notion of a Satan, and original sin developed. I can't pinpoint a specific reference, but I do want to honour her work.

Pagels Elaine. *Adam, Eve and the Serpent*, Random House, New York 1988.

_____ *Beyond Belief; The Secret Gospel of Thomas,* Vintage Books, New York, 2003.

_____ *The Gnostic Gospels,* Vintage Books, New York, 1979.

_____ *The Origin of Satan,* Vintage Books, New York, 1995.

Joseph Campbell

Joseph Campbell's extensive research into all of the world's myths reveals the commonality in themes, characters, and quests. Again, there is nothing specific I can reference, but he certainly has affirmed my growing awareness that we are all indeed — one.

Campbell, Joseph. *Creative Mythology; The Masks of God*, Penguin, New York, 1968.

_____ *The Hero with a Thousand Faces*, MJF Books, New York, 1949.

_____ *Thou Art That; Transforming Religious Metaphor*, New World Library, CA, 2001.

_____ *The Way of Myth; Talking with Joseph Campbell*, SHAMBALA, Boston & London, 1994.

William Pollock

During my graduate studies in theology and family therapy, I researched the dilemma that boys and men find themselves in. This book by Pollock is a helpful read for anyone working with boys. It is his phrase I reference in the chapter on Abraham, 'boys cry bullets'.

Pollock William. *Real Boys; Rescuing Our Sons from the Myths of Boyhood*, Owl Book, Henry Holt and Company, New York, 1999.

Riane Eisler

Eisler researches a time in ancient history when society was not ruled by a patriarchy. No weapons of war have been found on the archeological excavation site at Catal Huyuk, on the Isle of Crete. I reference this work in the chapter on creativity.

Eisler Riane. *The Chalice & The Blade; Our History, Our Future*, Harper, San Francisco, 1987.

Book of Thomas

I make two references to the Book of Thomas. In chapter three where Jesus says to lift up a stone and he is there, and on the last page of the chapter on Yeshua where the disciples asked Jesus what the end of the world would be like.

Robinson, James. *The Nag Hammadi Library: The definitive new translation of the Gnostic scriptures*, Harper, San Francisco, 1978.

David Korten

On the back cover of this book Joanna Macy, author of *Coming Back to Life* is quoted. "Here is a book we've been waiting for. We are not doomed to domination and suicidal competition. We can choose another story. This is the "Great Turning". And, of course, I say, "Yes, we most definitely can choose another story!" This book echoes the hope that I demonstrate in the latter part of our story. We absolutely can and should build the communities we want to live in, that value and respect everyone and all of Earth.

Korten, David. *The Great Turning; From Empire to Earth Community*, Burrett – Koehler Publishers, Inc., San Francisco, 2006.

Made in the USA
Charleston, SC
19 December 2012